Positive Psychology in a Nutshell

Positive Psychology in a nutshell

Positive Psychology in a Nutshell
The science of happiness
Third edition

Ilona Boniwell

Open University Press

Open University Press
McGraw-Hill Education
McGraw-Hill House
Shoppenhangers Road
Maidenhead
Berkshire
England
SL6 2QL

email: enquiries@openup.co.uk
world wide web: www.openup.co.uk

and Two Penn Plaza, New York, NY 10121-2289, USA

First edition published in 2006 by PWBC, London
Second edition published in 2008 by PWBC, London
This edition 2012

Copyright © Ilona Boniwell, 2012

Illustrations by Alexander Izotovs

A catalogue record of this book is available from the British Library

ISBN-13: 978-0-33-524720-2 (pb)
ISBN-10: 0-33-524720-2 (pb)
eISBN: 978-0-33-524721-9

Library of Congress Cataloging-in-Publication Data
CIP data applied for

Typesetting and e-book compilations by
RefineCatch Limited, Bungay, Suffolk
Printed and bound by CPI Group (UK) Ltd, Croydon, CR0 4YY

The McGraw·Hill Companies

Praise for the Second Edition:

"Positive Psychology in a Nutshell *is a comprehensive, user friendly, thoughtful introduction and critique of the field. Simply put, it is the best overview out there that can be read in a couple of sittings. Those with no psychology background find it fascinating and informative; those with serious credentials find it to be a credible overview and critique of the field.*"

Dr Carol Kauffman, Co-founder and Director of the Coaching and
Positive Psychology Initiative, Harvard Medical School, USA

"Positive Psychology in a Nutshell *is by far the best introduction to the topic. Great for the lay reader or professional.*"

Dr Carol Craig, Chief Executive, Centre for Confidence and
Well-being, Glasgow, UK

"This book does what the title suggests, and it does it well. If you want a sound introduction to the burgeoning field of positive psychology, read this... it would be useful for anyone – psychology student or anyone else – wanting to know about this area.*"

Professor Ben C. Fletcher, University of Hertfordshire, UK

"In a nutshell, I could scarcely put down this intelligent, balanced and irresistible introduction to positive psychology!*"

Dr Sean Cameron, Co-Director, Practitioner Doctorate in Educational
Psychology, University College London, UK

"Dr Ilona Boniwell's Positive Psychology in a Nutshell *is a beautifully written, clear and down-to-earth explanation of the essentials of a fast-growing and exciting new development in psychology. It is my number one introductory reference for students, applied psychologists, researchers and for those wanting to find out more about the topic.*"

Professor Irvine S. Gersch, Director of Educational
Psychology Programmes, University of East London, UK

Contents

Why I Wrote this Book   ix
Preface to the Third Edition   x
Acknowledgements   xi

1 What is Positive Psychology?   1

2 Your Emotions and You   9

3 Optimism and Hope   19

4 Living in Flow   29

5 Happiness and Subjective Well-being   37

6 Is Happiness Necessary or Sufficient? The Concept
   of Eudaimonic Well-being   49

7 Meaning in Making: Values, Motivation and
   Life Goals   63

8 Time in Our Lives   71

9 Positive Psychology and Life Complexities
   and Challenges   83

10 The Freedom of Choice and How to Survive it   95

11 The Positive Psychology of Strengths   103

12 Love   119

13 Positive Psychology Interventions   131

14 Putting it into Practice   143

15   The Future of Positive Psychology   161

     Internet Resources   169
     References   173
     Index   191

Why I Wrote this Book

As a founder of the European Network of Positive Psychology, leader of the first Masters in Applied Positive Psychology in Europe and a researcher, I am frequently asked to present an introductory lecture or a workshop on positive psychology. I have given talks to undergraduate and postgraduate students, managers, health professionals, educators and the general public. My talk usually generates a lot of excitement and interest. 'How can I learn a little bit more about it?' participants always ask. At this point, I usually pick up the 709-page *Oxford Handbook of Positive Psychology* and show it to the audience. It is generally met with silence, broken by an occasional giggle. Then I pick up the 598-page *Positive Psychology in Practice: The Scientific and Practical Explorations of Human Strengths*. It improves the situation but only slightly. Finally, I introduce the 270-page *Positive Psychology: Theory, Research and Applications* written by Kate Hefferon and myself, and about a third of my audience exhale with relief. For the other two-thirds this textbook, aimed at undergraduate psychology students, is still an unlikely read in our age of information overload.

This was the rationale behind the book you are holding now – to provide a concise but comprehensive introduction to positive psychology for an intelligent reader who is not necessarily a psychologist. Although it has 'tips and tools', this is not a self-help book but an attempt to offer a balanced account of what positive psychology is and what it is not, and what its strengths and its weaknesses are. It discusses many successes and discoveries, but also controversies within the field.

Much of what is inside the covers comes from reading books, scientific papers, going to conferences, talking to leading scholars and carrying out research. The book also draws on discussions with friends and colleagues, and questions raised by my students and the general audience. I hope this attempt to marry research findings with conceptual thinking and common sense produces a light but integrated perspective on positive psychology.

Preface to the Third Edition

Six years have passed since the first edition of this book, and nearly four since the second. The world of positive psychology has continued growing from strength to strength. As of 2012 we can talk of hundreds of undergraduate classes in American, European and British universities, with positive psychology being the most popular course in Harvard, attracting over a thousand students per semester. Today, the University of Pennsylvania and the University of East London are offering a Master in Applied Positive Psychology for those wishing to take their understanding and practice of positive psychology a step further, with many new Masters currently in the process of development in other countries. Modern positive psychology is no longer centred solely on its Philadelphia birthplace, as the new International Positive Psychology Association unites psychologists and practitioners around the world.

To my surprise and delight, the first two editions of this book were very well received. It has remained number one in the positive psychology listings on Amazon.co.uk for many years. With the book now being used by numerous lecturers for their courses, I have received positive feedback from many students and professionals even beyond psychology. People I had never met approached me at conferences and events to say how much they enjoyed reading it (it even got a mention at the launch of one report in the British Parliament).

As the time has come for a reprint, it became clear that some substantial elements are missing from the second edition. Today, when talking about positive psychology, it is virtually impossible not to mention research on mindsets and resilience. Furthermore, much more is known nowadays about the relationship between money and happiness, eudaimonic well-being and a balanced time perspective. Finally, with the explosion of printed and internet resources in the field, the recommended materials section has also been expanded substantially.

Acknowledgements

I gratefully acknowledge many friends and colleagues from the field of positive psychology for their direct and indirect contributions to this book (friendly discussions, correspondence and support that I have received from the Positive Psychology Network in the last eight years). Many thanks to: Philip Zimbardo, Anita Rogers, Alex Linley, Jane Henry, Ilona Roth, Susan David, Tim LeBon, Veronika Huta, James Pawelski, Barbara Fredrickson, Antonella Delle Fave, Felicia Huppert, Martin Seligman, Chris Peterson, George Vaillant, Edward Diener, Mihaly Csikszentmihalyi and Sheila Kearney.

Permissions

The author and the publisher gratefully acknowledge permission to reprint the following scales in this book:

- American Psychological Association and Rick Snyder for Adult Dispositional Hope Scale taken from Snyder, C.R., Harris, C., Anderson, J.R., Helleran, S.A., Irving, L.M., Sigmon, S.T., Yoshinobu, L., Gibb, J., Langelle, C., & Harney, P. (1991). The will and the ways: development and validation of an individual differences measure of hope. *Journal of Personality and Social Psychology*, 60, 570–585.
- Lawrence Erlbaum Associates, Inc. for Satisfaction With Life Scale taken from Diener, E., Emmons, R.A., Larson, R.J., & Griffin, S. (1985). The Satisfaction With Life Scale. *Journal of Personality Assessment*, 49, 71–75.

The author and the publisher gratefully acknowledge the VIA Institute for their permission to adapt Table 1.1 from Peterson, C., & Seligman,

M.E.P. (2005). *Character Strengths and Virtues: A Handbook and Classification*. Washington, DC: American Psychological Association.

Every effort has been made to trace copyright owners and anyone claiming copyright is advised to contact Editions Payot & Rivages.

Note

A final note before we begin: although in many places I use an expression 'he or she' when referring to a person/individual, in other parts of the book personal pronouns that indicate gender are used randomly. This is not reflective of any bias, but is done for purely practical reasons.

Chapter One

What is Positive Psychology?

You have probably heard of the term 'positive psychology' on TV, radio or even in fashion magazines. But what is it really? What does it stand for? Positive psychology is a science of positive aspects of human life, such as happiness, well-being and flourishing. It can be summarized in the words of its founder, Martin Seligman, as the 'scientific study of optimal human functioning [that] aims to discover and promote the factors that allow individuals and communities to thrive' (Seligman & Csikszentmihalyi, 2000).

Psychology has more often than not emphasized the shortcomings of individuals rather than their potentials. This particular approach focuses on the potentials. It is not targeted at fixing problems, but is focused on researching things that make life worth living instead. In short, positive psychology is concerned not with how to transform, for example, −8 to −2 but with how to bring +2 to +8.

This orientation in psychology was established about fourteen years ago and it is a rapidly developing field. Its aspiration is to bring solid empirical research into areas such as well-being, flow, personal strengths, wisdom, creativity, psychological health and characteristics of positive groups and institutions. The map overleaf shows the topics of interest for positive psychologists. This map is not, by any means, exhaustive, but it provides a good overview of the field and the book you are about to read.

Mind map of positive psychology

Three levels of positive psychology

The science of positive psychology operates on three different levels – the subjective level, the individual level and the group level.

The *subjective* level includes the study of positive experiences such as joy, well-being, satisfaction, contentment, happiness, optimism and flow. This level is about feeling good, rather than doing good or being a good person.

At the *individual* level, the aim is to identify the constituents of the 'good life' and the personal qualities that are necessary for being a 'good person', through studying human strengths and virtues, future-mindedness, capacity for love, courage, perseverance, forgiveness, originality, wisdom, interpersonal skills and giftedness.

Finally, at the *group or community* level, the emphasis is on civic virtues, social responsibilities, nurturance, altruism, civility, tolerance, work ethics, positive institutions and other factors that contribute to the development of citizenship and communities and reaching beyond oneself. This level is much more about taking actions or positive behaviours aimed at something larger than ourselves.

This book will mainly concentrate on the first two levels, but Chapter 14 ('Putting it into practice') will touch upon the third one.

Why do we have positive psychology?

According to positive psychologists, for most of its life mainstream psychology (sometimes also referred to as 'psychology as usual') has been concerned with the negative aspects of human life. There have been pockets of interest in topics such as creativity, optimism and wisdom, but they have not been united behind any grand theory or a broad, over-arching framework. This rather negative state of affairs was not the original intention of the first psychologists, but came about through a historical accident. Before the Second World War, psychology had three tasks: to cure mental illness, to improve normal lives and to identify and nurture high talent. However, after the War the last two tasks somehow got lost, leaving the field to concentrate predominantly on the first one (Seligman & Csikszentmihalyi, 2000). How did that happen? Given that psychology as a science depends heavily on the funding of governmental bodies, it is not hard to assume what happened to the resources after the War. Understandably, facing a human crisis on such an enormous scale, all available resources were poured into learning about, and the treatment of, psychological illness and psychopathology.

This is how psychology as a field learnt to operate within a *disease model*. This model has proven very useful. Seligman highlights the victories of the disease model, which are, for example, that fourteen previously incurable mental illnesses (including depression, personality disorder and anxiety attacks) can now be successfully treated. However, the costs of adopting this disease model included the negative view of psychologists as 'victimologists' and 'pathologizers', the failure to address the improvement of normal lives and the identification and nurturance of high talent. Just to illustrate, if you were to say to your friends that you were going to see a psychologist, their most likely response would be: 'What's wrong with you?' You're unlikely to hear something along the lines of: 'Great! Are you planning to concentrate on self-improvement?'

Many psychologists admit that we have little knowledge of what makes life worth living or of how normal people flourish under usual, rather than extreme, conditions. In fact, we often have little more to say about the good life than self-help gurus. But shouldn't we know better? The Western world has long outgrown the rationale for an exclusively disease model of psychology. Perhaps now is the time to redress the balance by using psychology resources to learn about normal and flourishing lives, rather than lives that are in need of help. Perhaps now is the time to gather knowledge about strengths and talents, high achievement (in every sense of this word), the best ways and means of self-improvement, fulfilling work and relationships, and a great art of ordinary living carried out in every corner of the planet. This is the rationale behind the creation of positive psychology.

However, positive psychology is still nothing else but psychology, adopting the same scientific method. It simply studies different (and often far more interesting) topics and asks slightly different questions, such as 'what works?' rather than 'what doesn't?' or 'what is right with this person?' rather than 'what is wrong?'

Aren't we reinventing the wheel? The historical roots of positive psychology

Positive psychology places great emphasis on being a new and forward-thinking discipline. While the second claim might be true, the idea as such is hardly new. The roots of positive psychology can be traced to the thoughts of ancient Greek philosophers. Aristotle believed that there was a unique *daimon*, or spirit, within each individual that guides us to pursue things that are right for us. Acting in accordance with this daimon leads one to happiness. The question of happiness has since been picked up by hundreds, if not thousands, of prominent thinkers, and has given rise to many theories, including Hedonism, with its emphasis on pleasure, and Utilitarianism, seeking the greatest happiness for the greatest number.

While Western philosophical thought is undoubtedly a major influence on the subject matter of positive psychology, another influence that is rarely acknowledged comes from the Eastern traditions of Hinduism and Buddhism. Love, kindness, compassion and joy, which are the emotions explicitly promoted by these traditions as paths to happiness, are in themselves major areas of research in modern positive psychology. Various Buddhist approaches offer many different methods for cultivating positive emotions. Nowadays, many of these practices and techniques, such as yoga, mindfulness and meditation, claim a prominent place in the field of positive psychology, having undergone randomized controlled studies.

In the twentieth century, many prominent psychologists focused on what later became the subject matter of positive psychology. Among them were: Carl Jung, with his individuation, or 'becoming all that one can be', concept (Jung, 1933); Maria Jahoda, concerned with defining positive mental health (Jahoda, 1958); and Gordon Allport, interested in individual maturity (Allport, 1955), while the matters of flourishing and well-being were raised in the work on prevention (see, for example, Cowen et al., 1967) and wellness enhancement (Cowen, 1994). The most notable of positive psychology's predecessors, however, was the humanistic psychology movement, which originated in the 1950s and reached its peak in the 1960s and 1970s. This movement placed central emphasis on the growth and authentic self of an individual. Humanistic psychologists were critical of pathology-oriented approaches to a human being. The most famous among them were Carl Rogers, who introduced the concept of the fully functioning person, and Abraham Maslow, who emphasized self-actualization. In fact, it was Maslow who was the very first psychologist to use the term 'positive psychology'.

Humanistic psychologists, however, did not only reject the dominant negative paradigm of psychology, they also believed that the so-called 'scientific method' (good for studying molecules and atoms) helps little in understanding the human being in its complexity and called for more qualitative rather than quantitative (statistical, number crunching) research. This is where positive psychology disagrees with its major predecessor. Positive psychology believes that humanistic psychology, because of its scepticism of an empirical method, is not very grounded scientifically. Contrary to the humanists, while rejecting the mainstream psychology preoccupation with negative topics, positive psychology embraces the dominant scientific paradigm. Positive psychology thus distinguishes itself from humanistic psychology on the basis of methods (Peterson & Seligman, 2004), whereas the substance and the topics studied are remarkably similar. Rightly or wrongly, positive psychology tends to present itself as a new movement, often attempting to distance itself from its origins.

The roots of positive psychology

Further reading

Gable, S.L., & Haidt, J. (2005). What (and why) is positive psychology? *Review of General Psychology*, 9, 103–110.

Seligman, M.E.P., & Csikszentmihalyi, M. (2000). Positive psychology: An introduction. *American Psychologist*, 55, 5–14.

Chapter Two
Your Emotions and You

The term 'emotion' is notoriously difficult to define. As Fehr and Russell put it: 'everyone knows what emotion is until asked to give a definition' (Oatley & Jenkins, 1996: 96). Yet we all use this term and seem to easily understand to what, in our experience, it relates. Psychologists often employ the notion of affect[1] as an umbrella term for various positive and negative emotions, feelings and moods we frequently experience and easily recognize. In this chapter, I consider two 'affective' topics popular within positive psychology – positive emotions and emotional intelligence.

The value of positive emotions

For years, psychology turned its attention to the study of negative emotions or negative affect, including depression, sadness, anger, stress and anxiety. Not surprisingly, psychologists found them interesting because they may often lead to, or signal the presence of, psychological disorders. However, positive emotions are no less fascinating, if only because of many common-sense misconceptions that exist about positive affect. We tend to think, for example, that positive affect typically, by its very nature, distorts or disrupts orderly, effective thinking, that positive emotions are somehow 'simple' or that, because these emotions are short-lived, they cannot have a long-term impact. Research has shown the above not to be the case, but it took it a while to get there (Isen, 2002). It is only relatively recently that psychologists realized that positive emotions can be seen as valuable in their own right and started studying them.

The person behind that realization was Barbara Fredrickson, who devoted most of her academic career to trying to understand the benefits of the positive emotions. The functions of negative emotions have been clear for some time. Negative emotions, such as anxiety or anger, are associated with tendencies to act in specific ways, which are adaptive in evolutionary terms (e.g. the fight and flight response). Thus, fear contributes to a tendency to escape and anger to a tendency to attack. If our ancestors were not equipped with such effective emotional tools, our own existence might have been in doubt. Moreover, negative emotions seem to narrow our action repertoires (or actual behaviours) – when running from danger, we are unlikely to appreciate a beautiful sunset. This function of negative emotions can help minimize distractions in an acute situation. Positive emotions, on the other hand, are not associated with specific actions. So what good are they, apart from the fact that they merely feel good? What is the point in feeling happy or joyful, affectionate or ecstatic?

The 'broaden-and-build' theory of positive emotions, developed by Barbara Fredrickson, shows that positive affective experiences contribute to and have a long-lasting effect on our personal growth and development (Fredrickson, 2001). And this is how they do it:

(a) *Positive emotions broaden our thought–action repertoires*
First, positive emotions broaden our attention and thinking, which means that we have more positive thoughts and a greater variety of them. When we are experiencing positive emotions, such as joy or interest, we are more likely to be creative, to see more opportunities, to be open to relationships with others, to play, to be more flexible and open-minded.

(b) *Positive emotions undo negative emotions*
It's hard to experience both positive and negative emotions simultaneously; thus a deliberate experience of positive emotions at times when

negative emotions are dominant can serve to undo their lingering effects. Mild joy and contentment can eliminate the stress experienced at a physiological level.

(c) *Positive emotions enhance resilience*
Enjoyment, happy playfulness, contentment, satisfaction, warm friendship, love and affection, all enhance resilience and the ability to cope, while negative emotions, in contrast, decrease them. Positive emotions can enhance problem-focused coping and reappraisal, or infuse negative events with positive meaning, all of which facilitate fast bouncing back after an unpleasant event.

(d) *Positive emotions build psychological repertoire*
Far from having only a momentary effect, positive emotions help to build important physical, intellectual, social and psychological resources

The resilience hypothesis

that are enduring, even though the emotions themselves are temporary. For example, the positive emotions associated with play can build physical abilities; self-mastery and enjoyable times with friends increase social skills.

(e) *Positive emotions can trigger an upward developmental spiral*
More than that, just as negative emotions can lead one into downward spirals of depression, positive emotions can trigger upward developmental spirals towards improved emotional well-being and transform people into better versions of themselves.

The broaden-and-build theory urges us to consider positive emotions not as an end in themselves but as a means of leading a better life. Positive emotions are distinguished from temporary pleasant sensations such as eating chocolate ice cream, drinking beer, doing drugs or getting a massage. These sensations are not the same as positive emotions, since they do not lead to the accumulation of durable personal resources.

Tips & Tools
How can we increase positive emotions?
The emotion of contentment can be enhanced by engaging in relaxation practices, such as progressive muscle relaxation, yoga and imagery exercises. Meditation exercises help achieve a state of mindfulness, which brings many other benefits (Fredrickson, 2001).

A lot of interesting research highlights the benefits of positive emotions. In one study with people who had lost their partners, researchers found that laughter and Duchenne smiling predicts the duration of grief. A Duchenne smile is a genuine smile characterized by the corners of the mouth turning up and crinkling of the skin around the corners of the eyes. People who laughed and smiled genuinely were more likely to be engaged in life and dating again two and a half years later, compared with those who felt angry (Keltner & Bonanno, 1997).

A famous yearbook study traced the lives of women who were attending an all-women's college in 1965. The faces of the women in their college photographs were coded for smiling behaviour and results showed that Duchenne smiles related to less negativity, greater competence, more positive ratings from others and greater well-being in their later lives (Harker & Keltner, 2001). Although a follow-up study that adopted a slightly different coding procedure did not manage to replicate all of the findings (Freese et al., 2006), more recent research has demonstrated that the absence of smiling in childhood photographs almost certainly predicts divorce (Hertenstein et al. 2009). Another study found that physicians experiencing positive emotions seem to make more accurate diagnoses (Isen et al., 1991).

Tips & Tools
Finding positive meaning
We can't simply will ourselves to feel a particular emotion, nor can anyone instil it in us. Even engaging in pleasant activities does not guarantee positive emotions, because they depend on our interpretations. What we can do is make an effort to find positive meaning in our daily activities by reframing them in positive terms or discovering a positive value in these activities (Fredrickson, 2002).

Let us not throw the baby out with the bath water – the positive impact of negative emotions

So how much positivity do we need to have for a truly thriving existence? It appears that the ratio of 3:1 or above of positivity to negativity results in the experience of flourishing, and anything below this ratio (e.g. 2:1) in the experience of languishing (Fredrickson, 2004). So make sure that for every one negative emotion, you have at least three positive ones. But beware: too much of even the best thing can be simply dangerous. Experiencing positivity at above 8:1 can have counterproductive effects.

Positive emotions can certainly help us on the rocky path to well-being but that does not make the negative emotions irrelevant or unimportant. They may not feel quite as good, but they can bring about very positive effects nevertheless. In defence of negative emotions, I propose the following:

- Negative emotions can help initiate fundamental personality changes. A leading expert on emotions, Richard Lazarus, writes: 'For the stable adult, major personality change may require a trauma, a personal crisis, or a religious conversion' (2003a: 105).
- Negative emotions can bring us to our depth and put us in touch with our deeper selves.
- They can facilitate learning, understanding of ourselves and knowledge of the world. Wisdom is often gained from experiencing suffering and loss that are the necessary parts of life (Young-Eisendrath, 2003).
- Finally, experiencing and coping with negative affect can have positive social consequences, such as modesty, moral considerations, care and empathy.

Some scholars think that putting all the emotions into two loose bags of positive and negative is hardly a wise move. Hope, for example, is best conceived as a combination of a wish that a desired outcome will occur with anxiety that it might not. What is it then – a positive or a negative emotion? Pride is generally regarded as a positive emotion in the West but seen to be a sin in more collectivistic societies. Love, one of the first emotions to spring to mind when mentioning the positive, is hardly such when unrequited. Can smiling and laughing be considered positive emotions when directed at someone (Campos, 2003)? What we shouldn't underestimate while trying to understand emotions is that what often makes them negative or positive is the context within which they occur (Lazarus, 2003a).

Emotional intelligence

'Emotional intelligence', or EQ, is a well-known term, popularized (though not invented) by Daniel Goleman (1995) in his bestseller *Emotional Intelligence: Why it can Matter More than IQ*. Little could the academics John Mayer and Peter Salovey, who studied this subject well before Goleman's book was published (e.g. Mayer et al., 1990; Salovey & Mayer, 1990), know that by allowing Goleman to use their term, he, rather than they, would be crowned with 'discovering' emotional intelligence.

Emotional intelligence refers to the capacity to recognize and manage our own emotions and the emotions of others close to us. It is often claimed to be more important than IQ for career success and for achievement of one's life goals.

With the explosion of the EQ phenomenon, much thinking and research has been carried out around the concept and, as a result, multiple models of EQ have been advocated. Here, I outline the Mayer-Salovey-Caruso model as an example of the better-developed ones. It proposes that there are four major branches or facets to the emotional intelligence concept (Salovey et al., 2004).

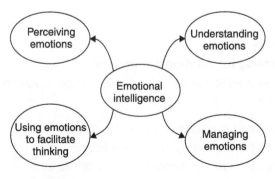

The four branches of EQ

1. Perceiving emotions

This is an ability to identify emotional messages in facial expressions, tone of voice and even works of art. People who are skilled at perceiving emotions in themselves and others have an advantage in social situations, as they are more likely to understand things from another person's perspective and are more empathic.

2. Using emotions to facilitate thinking

Emotions have the power to change the way we think. When we are happy we may think that everything is possible, whereas when we are sad we tend to have more negative thoughts. This branch is about how emotions affect our thinking and how we can utilize our emotions for more effective problem-solving, reasoning, decision-making and creative endeavours.

3. Understanding emotions

It's not enough to notice emotions – we need to figure out the message they are carrying. Why do we have certain emotions? Where are they coming from? What are they likely to lead us to? It's important to understand, for example, that irritation may lead to anger; or feeling insecure, to unpredictable outbursts. Emotionally intelligent individuals are capable of labelling emotions with words appropriately, and also of understanding complex feelings and even contradictory emotional states.

Tips & Tools
Self-monitoring for emotional awareness

Keep a mood diary to monitor what causes changes in your mood. Note the following:

- The **A**dversity that caused your mood to change
- The **B**eliefs that caused your mood to change
- The **C**onsequent mood change on a scale of 1 to 10

This knowledge will help you understand your emotions and start gaining control over them (Carr, 2004). You can take this exercise two steps further to challenge the beliefs that brought your mood down:

- The **D**isputation – try to think of alternative beliefs to explain the adversity and then notice . . .
- The **E**nergy change on a scale of 1 to 10.

4. *Managing emotions*

Emotional management or regulation is not about eliminating troubling emotions (life would be limited if this was the case), but about learning how to gain control over them. Some of us, when upset, think there is nothing that we can do about it; others believe that they can do something to make themselves feel better. Successful emotion-managers are often capable of helping others to deal with their emotions too.

Tips & Tools

Emotional management – what works well

- Expenditure of energy (e.g. physical exercise)
- Cognitive effort (e.g. giving yourself a 'pep-talk')
- Active mood management (such as relaxation and music)
- Social interactions
- Pleasant distractions (e.g. hobbies, shopping, errands)

Emotional management – what is less effective

- Direct stress and tension reduction (e.g. drugs and alcohol)
- Avoiding the person or thing that caused a bad mood
- Passive mood management (e.g. TV, coffee, food and sleep)
- Spending time alone (Salovey et al., 2002)

Separation of these EQ branches seems to make sense when we apply these findings to real life. A person may be skilled at listening to people, feeling for them and even understanding them, yet fail to make good contact with others simply because he or she cannot 'read' non-verbal cues. Thus, perceiving emotions may be precisely the area where intervention is needed in this case (Salovey et al., 2004).

The concept of emotional intelligence, however, is not without its problems. There is much debate about which branches should be in or out, whether emotional intelligence is really about emotions rather than our ability to rationally conceptualize them, and what the best way to measure EQ is. Still, emotional intelligence seems to offer useful insights into the convoluted and complex inner worlds of human beings.

Note

1 Some researchers make a distinction between emotions and affect, treating affect as broader and longer-lasting, but in this book I will use these notions interchangeably.

Further reading

Fredrickson, B. (2009). *Positivity*. New York: Crown.

Chapter Three
Optimism and Hope

A story about optimists and pessimists

People can be differentiated to the extent that they have different *expectancies* about the achievement of their goals, and other future events. *Optimists* have a generalized sense of confidence about the future, characterized by their broad expectancy that outcomes are likely to be positive. *Pessimists*, on the other hand, have a generalized sense of doubt and hesitancy, characterized by their anticipation of negative outcomes. So is it better to be an optimist or a pessimist?

Why it is good to be an optimist

Positive psychology research has found many advantages of adopting an optimistic viewpoint. Here are some of them:

- Optimists experience less distress than pessimists when dealing with difficulties in their lives. For example, they suffer much less anxiety and depression.
- Optimists adapt better to negative events (including coronary artery bypass surgery, breast cancer, abortion, bone marrow transplantation and AIDS).
- Optimism protects new mothers against developing depression following the birth of their baby.
- Optimism is conducive to problem-focused coping, humour, making plans, positive reframing (putting the situation in the best

19

possible light) and, when the situation is uncontrollable, accepting the reality of the situation. Optimists are capable of learning lessons from negative situations. Thus optimists have a coping advantage over pessimists.

- Perhaps surprisingly, optimists don't tend to use denial, whereas pessimists often attempt to distance themselves from the problem. Optimists are not simply people who stick their heads in the sand and ignore threats to their well-being. For example, they attend to health warnings and usually discover potentially serious problems earlier rather than later.

- Optimists exert more continuous effort and tend not to give up, possibly assuming that the situation can be handled successfully in one way or another. Pessimists, on the other hand, are far more likely to anticipate disaster – and, as a result, are more likely to give up.

- Optimists report more health-promoting behaviours (like eating a healthy diet or having regular medical check-ups) and enjoy better physical health than pessimists.

- Optimists seem to be more productive in the workplace (Robbins et al., 1991; Carver & Scheier, 2002).

Furthermore, over the past century, 85 per cent of US presidential elections were won by the more optimistic candidate (Zullow et al., 1988) – which, however, does not necessarily mean the best candidate! The conclusions of one insurance sales study contain a warning for pessimistic salespersons. Apparently, when the salespeople scoring in the top 10 per cent in an optimism questionnaire were compared with those scoring in the bottom 10 percent, it transpired that the former sold 88 per cent more insurance (Seligman & Schulman, 1986).

Can optimism be learnt?

Quite simply – yes. Although there may well be a genetically inherited component to optimism, and early childhood experiences certainly shape our optimistic–pessimistic viewpoint, we can use several strategies to counter pessimism.

The first of these is a *disputing* strategy, introduced by Martin Seligman (1991) in his bestseller *Learned Optimism*. We usually employ the skill of internal disputing when we are falsely accused of something by another person. We think to ourselves, for example: 'That's not right. It's him who is not listening, it's not me. I always listen before reaching a conclusion.' However, when we falsely accuse ourselves of something (e.g. not being capable of dealing with a difficult situation), we don't tend to dispute it. The key to success is careful monitoring and recognition of our thoughts. Once a negative thought is detected, we can consciously dispute that thought and try to look at possible alternative outcomes.

Changing and monitoring your *explanatory style* is another useful strategy. Explanatory style refers to the way in which we explain the causes and influences of previous positive and negative events.

A pessimistic explanatory style means we use internal, stable and global explanations for bad events, and external, unstable and specific explanations for good ones. People who use this style tend to appraise bad events in terms of personal failure.

An optimistic explanatory style, on the other hand, is characterized by external (leaving one's self-esteem intact), unstable and specific (depending on circumstances) explanations for bad events, and by the opposite pattern for good ones. Table 3.1 gives some examples of optimistic and pessimistic explanatory styles.

Needless to say, Seligman recommends monitoring your automatic thoughts and attitudes and disputing pessimistic explanations.

TABLE 3.1 OPTIMISTIC AND PESSIMISTIC EXPLANATORY STYLES

EVENT	OPTIMIST WOULD SAY:	PESSIMIST WOULD SAY:
Good event (e.g. passing an exam)	*Internal:* I've done a great job. *Stable:* I am talented. *Global:* This was a good start to the exam season. The other ones should be easy too.	*External:* Don't know how this happened. It must've been luck. *Unstable:* Every dog has its day. *Specific:* So what? I can still fail the next one.
Bad event (e.g. failing an exam)	*External:* The exam questions were simply terrible. *Unstable:* No problem, I'll pass it next time round. *Specific:* Yesterday was my birthday after all.	*Internal:* It's all my fault, I haven't prepared well. *Stable:* I am never going to pass this exam. *Global:* This is the end to my dreams; I'll never become who I want to be.

Tips & Tools
When disputing pessimistic explanations . . .
ask yourself what *evidence* you have for your beliefs. See if you can find
an *alternative* explanation for failure. Even if an optimistic explanation is
not applicable, what are the *implications* of this adversity? Is it really
that catastrophic? If you cannot decide which explanation is more valid,
think which one is more *useful* for your mood (Carr, 2004).

During lectures on this subject, at the point when I have nearly sold optimism as well as the positive attribution style to my listeners, I am usually met with a variation on the following question: 'Surely you are not saying that blaming anyone else but yourself when things go wrong is a good idea?' This is a very good question. The research that I know of does not seem to tackle the impact of an optimistic explanatory style on those close to the optimists, nor does it report on whether optimism is associated with qualities such as self-centredness.

Why it is good to be a pessimist

There are occasions when pessimism can do more to ensure the safety of your life. Optimistic thinking is associated with an underestimation of risks (Peterson & Park, 2003), so optimists are more likely to take part in high-risk activities such as unprotected sex or reckless driving. Optimism is also hardly desirable if, for example, a pilot is deciding whether a plane should take off during an ice-storm.

In the case of serious traumatic events (e.g. death, fire, flood or violent rape), optimists may not be well prepared and their beautiful, rosy world may be shattered into pieces (although optimists might be better equipped to rebuild it than pessimists).

Furthermore, research has found that there is a type of pessimist who hardly ever benefits from learning how to be optimistic and adopting a positive mood. This characteristic is called 'defensive pessimism'. It is a cognitive strategy to set low expectations for upcoming performance, despite having performed well previously in similar circumstances. Defensive pessimists use the expectation that things will turn out badly as a coping mechanism: they perform better when they're allowed to imagine what could go wrong and keep hold of their low expectations. Defensive pessimism helps anxious people manage their anxiety and, contrary to what you might think, trying to be optimistic actually makes their performance worse! Over time, defensive pessimists start feeling better about themselves, become happier, perform better academically and make more progress on their personal goals than equally anxious people who do not use defensive pessimism (Norem & Chang, 2002).

What about realism?

This is another difficult question to answer, simply because realism does not seem to be in fashion at the moment. Having carefully analysed the indexes of five major volumes on positive psychology, I found only one reference to this term.

If a principal motivation of a realist is to understand themselves and the world as it is and to maintain a consistent and accurate self-image, it would be common sense to assume that such a disposition could benefit from the strengths of both optimism and pessimism, while avoiding the pitfalls associated with both.

Ed Diener (2003), one of the greatest researchers on happiness, writes: 'it might not be desirable for an individual to be too optimistic; perhaps people are better off if they are a mix of optimism and pessimism' (p. 117). Barbara Ehrenreich (2010), probably the most prominent critic of the positive psychology movement, goes much further to suggest that it is the positive or optimistic thinking that may actually be responsible for the banking crisis, for making some chronic illnesses worse, and for the enormous amounts of money spent on 'improving' ourselves when the real impediments to happiness lie far beyond our control.

Perhaps our Western societies need some realists: people who follow current affairs, feel for the suffering around the world and assume some responsibility for the causes and implications of this adversity. People who choose to do something about it, despite their limited chances of success.

But then again, at least some optimism seems necessary to motivate us to take the very next step forward. Sandra Schneider writes at length about realistic vs. unrealistic optimism, stressing the difference between 'fuzzy' knowledge and 'fuzzy' meaning, and the importance of reality checks. Fuzzy knowledge is about not knowing the facts, while fuzzy meaning is about having some latitude in interpretations. Optimism is not a good way to deal with fuzzy knowledge. If you don't know your level of cholesterol, it doesn't make sense to just assume you are safe from cardiac disease. However, many situations in life are, in fact, open to interpretation – and this is where optimism can be useful (Schneider, 2001). In fact, both Schneider's and Seligman's approaches advocate the same principle – that of flexibility of thinking when it comes to interpreting the meaning of events. It is hardly surprising, therefore, that many resilience programmes (see Chapter 14) are based on the theories of optimism, teaching students to question their habitual explanations for misfortunes.

Tips & Tools
Positive realism or realistic optimism?
Blind optimism may result in carelessness and unrealistic expectations, which is unproductive in the long run. This can be avoided if you don't allow wishful thinking to influence your judgements. Being positive is compatible with being realistic. It does not mean expecting only positive outcomes, but having confidence that even if things don't go your way, you will be able to deal with the situation (or even somehow benefit from it) (Popovic, 2005).

Goals Scale

Completing this questionnaire may tell you something about yourself. It is explained more fully after the box, but if you decide to fill it in, don't look until you have actually done so.

Directions: Read each question carefully. Using the scale shown below, please select the number that best describes YOU and put this number in the blank provided.

1 = Definitely False
2 = Mostly False
3 = Mostly True
4 = Definitely True

____ 1. I can think of many ways to get out of a jam.
____ 2. I energetically pursue my goals.
____ 3. I feel tired most of the time.
____ 4. There are lots of ways around my problem.
____ 5. I am easily downed in an argument.
____ 6. I can think of many ways to get things in life that are most important to me.
____ 7. I worry about my health.
____ 8. Even when others get discouraged, I know I can find a way to solve the problem.
____ 9. My past experiences have prepared me well for my future.
____ 10. I've been pretty successful in life.
____ 11. I usually find myself worrying about something.
____ 12. I meet the goals that I set for myself.

Now add together your scores for Questions 1, 2, 4, 6, 8, 9, 10 and 12, and read on.

You have just filled in the questionnaire on hope (Lopez et al., 2004). Your score, which will range from 8 to 32, should show how hopeful you are. Don't worry about Questions 3, 5, 7 and 11 – they are simply distracters and should not be counted towards the final result. Read on to find out how positive psychology views hope and what can be done to increase it.

Is there any hope?

Hope is a construct that is closely related to optimism, although the two are not identical. Rick Snyder, one of the leading specialists in hope, represents it as an ability to conceptualize goals, find pathways to these goals despite obstacles and have the motivation to use those pathways (Lopez et al., 2004). To put it more simply, we feel hopeful if we: (a) know what we want, (b) can think of a range of ways to get there and (c) start and keep on going.

Pathway thinking, or generating several workable routes to the goal, is very important because a particular route may not always be the best. Even if the main route is blocked, a hopeful person will find other options open to him or her. Questions 1, 4, 6 and 8 of the Goals Scale measured your pathways score. However, knowing how to go about something is not enough, you need to get moving! This is where agency thoughts (such as 'I can do this', 'I won't be stopped') come into play. Motivation is not only about starting, it's also about staying energized and 'on task'. Questions 2, 9, 10 and 12 measured your motivation or agency.

It's not hard to see that being hopeful brings about many benefits. For example, we know that hope buffers against interfering, self-deprecatory thoughts and negative emotions, and is critical for psychological health. In the domain of physical health, we know that people who are hopeful focus more on the prevention of diseases (e.g. through exercising). Athletes with higher levels of hope are more successful in their performance. Furthermore, based on research with college students, it appears that hope bears a substantial relationship to academic achievement (Snyder et al., 2002).

Snyder and his colleagues (2002) emphasize a cognitive rather than an emotional approach to hope, claiming that positive emotions are the result of concluding that we are pursuing goals successfully. This means that they see hope as a goal-pursuit thinking that causes emotions. As often happens in psychology, many other researchers would not subscribe to this view, conceptualizing hope as an emotion in itself (Farina et al., 1995).

Tips & Tools

Let's hope

To generate hope, first formulate your goals, think of several ways of how these can be achieved and select the best one, break your goals into smaller sub-goals, motivate yourself to pursue your goals and reframe any obstacles you meet as challenges to be overcome (Carr, 2004).

On 7 July 2005, I was in Central London, stopping frequently to catch the latest news about the four explosions in the city and responding to multiple phone calls from family and friends, checking to see if I was okay. In the midst of this nightmare, with images of buses without their tops and reports of people still stuck in the Underground, I am not optimistic about the future. Having learnt from the post-September 11 trajectory, I can see the rise in the psychology of fear on English soil, anti-terrorist measures dominating the media, and the celebrated multiculturalism of London descending into hatred and suspicion towards the Muslim population. Yet I am hopeful. Hopeful that everything will be alright in the end, despite the fact that I do not know what this 'alright' may look like, how we can get there and whether I personally can do anything about it. As far as I can see, my experience of the present moment is stripped of both being able to envisage the pathways and of feeling that my personal agency can have much effect on the final and very unclear outcome. In spite of that, I still feel the emotion of hope, which remains even in contradiction to the theory I have just described above.

Further reading

Seligman, M.E.P. (1991). *Learned optimism*. New York: Knopf.

Chapter Four
Living in Flow

Have you ever spent what you thought was half an hour searching the internet, only to find out afterwards that your session lasted three hours? Or opened a book shortly after breakfast and a little while later noticed that it was getting darker?

Think of a moment in your life when you were so involved in what you were doing that the rest of the world seemed to have disappeared. Your mind wasn't wandering; you were totally focused and concentrated on that activity, to such an extent that you were not even aware of yourself. Time disappeared too. Only when you came out of the experience did you realize how much time had actually passed (usually much more than you anticipated, although sometimes less).

Most people can remember experiencing such a state. In fact, about 90 per cent can associate such a state with one or more activities. Athletes call it 'being in the zone', others a 'heightened state of consciousness'. Psychologists call these fully absorbing experiences *flow states*, which were discovered and named by a world-famous psychologist with the most unpronounceable surname I have ever encountered – Mihaly Csikszentmihalyi.[1] His celebrated book, *Flow: The Psychology of Happiness*, is one of the best examples of a marriage between non-reductionist scientific and deep thinking, within the accessible self-help genre. It became an instant bestseller, making its way to the top of the self-help classics.[2]

It is possible that if it wasn't for the enormous popularity of *Flow* and for Seligman and Csikszentmihalyi meeting accidentally in Hawaii and becoming friends (Seligman, 2002), the positive psychology movement might never have been born.

Making flow happen

The state of flow happens under very specific conditions – when we encounter a challenge that tests our skills, and yet our skills and capacities are such that it is just about possible to meet that challenge. So both the challenge and the skills are at high levels, stretching us almost to the limit.

If challenges exceed skills, one can become anxious. If skills exceed challenges, we usually become bored (like bright kids at school). Neither of these two cases results in flow.

Csikszentmihalyi (1992) investigated the phenomenon of flow by interviewing thousands of people from many different walks of life – chess players, mountain climbers, tennis players, ballet dancers, surgeons, and so on. He came to the conclusion that flow is a universal experience, which has several important characteristics:

- *Clarity of goals and immediate feedback on progress.* For example, in a competition you know what you've got to achieve and you know exactly how well you are doing, i.e. whether you are winning or losing.
- *Complete concentration* on what one is doing at the present moment, with no room in one's mind for any other information.
- *Actions and awareness are merged.* A guitar player merges with his instrument and becomes the music that he plays. The activity seemingly becomes automatic, and the involvement effortless – though this is far from the truth.
- *Losing awareness of oneself or self-consciousness* is also a common experience but, interestingly, after each flow experience the sense of self is strengthened and a person becomes more than he or she was before.

- *Sense of control* over what one is doing, with no worries about failure.
- *Transformation of time.* Usually, time passes much faster than expected. However, the reverse can also be true.
- *Activities are intrinsically rewarding.* This means they have an end in themselves (you do something because you want to), with any other goal often being just an excuse.

What is also interesting in flow is the almost total absence of emotions during the actual process. One seems to be almost beyond experiencing emotions, most likely because the awareness of self is not present. It is important to note, however, that we experience an increase in positive emotions after the occurrence of flow (Seligman, 2002).

Popovic (? Nash, personal communication) describes his own experience of flow as follows:

> A good discussion often brings a sense of flow. I am not aware of myself, the world around, or the passage of time. I get totally involved in the conversation. Everything goes smoothly. It is a challenging but not a rough ride. Yet, like with all truly fulfilling experiences, you know that you were in flow, not while you were there, but because of missing it after.

Thinking about it, it seems to me that the merger between a person and his or her own action, coupled with complete concentration, enables that person to spend less energy on an activity than it would usually require and therefore achieve more with less effort. An increased effort is necessary to get us into this state, but once there, an activity feels almost effortless. As such, flow can be conceptualized as a *low-energy solution to high-energy problems*.

Activities that lead to a flow experience are called *autotelic* (from the Greek: *auto* = self, *telos* = goal), because they are intrinsically motivated and enjoyable and have an end in themselves, rather than in some other end product.

Many activities are conducive to flow: sports, dancing, involvement in creative arts and other hobbies, sex, socializing, studying, reading and, very often, working. In fact, most daily activities can lead to *optimal experience* (another name for flow), as long as the situation is sufficiently complex to activate the high-challenge, high-skill condition (Della Fave & Massimini, 2004a). Activities in which flow is rarely experienced include housework, idling and resting. In addition, in most cultures, people don't associate watching TV with optimal experience.

Although optimal experience is described in the same way across countries, some of the flow-conducive activities vary, because of cultural and circumstantial differences. Thus Roma (Gypsy) people very often find flow in raising children or grandchildren, which is not a common pattern elsewhere. Leisure activities, which are frequently associated with optimal experience, are not associated with them in Iran. People in traditional societies find flow in housework, though this is rare in Europe (Della Fave & Massimini, 2004b). Perhaps, it is the societal perception of housework as a somewhat inferior activity that may have something to do with it. While TV is generally counter-productive for flow, blind people quote media (including television 'watching') as their most flow-related activity. This is not surprising: TV is not designed for blind people, so 'watching' TV is for them associated with a challenge – having to build mental images of the characters in the absence of being able to see them. Nepalese people, too, associate the media with optimal experience. Not having a TV at home makes watching it a rare (and possibly challenging) opportunity (Della Fave & Massimini, 2004a). These research findings mean it is not possible to say for certain which activities are definitely flow-related and which are not. What for one person is 'a piece of cake' can be a challenge for another. The opportunities for optimal experience rely, therefore, on our subjective perception.

Having said that, the frequent choice of activities that are non-conducive to flow is a problem for the majority in the West. Remember, it is not just the balance between challenge and skills that is necessary for flow – both have to be stretched. When watching TV, for example, the low skill matches the low challenge, which usually results in apathy, unless, of course, we are watching a documentary on quantum mechanics. At work, on the other hand, we experience high-skill, high-challenge situations more often than during leisure. Yet we often would rather do something else than work. Given a choice between TV and work, why would we choose the former over the latter? Csikszentmihalyi explains this by distinguishing between enjoyment and pleasures. Flow may be a state of ultimate enjoyment, but it requires effort and work, at least to begin with. It's far too easy to switch the TV on, and it is this effortlessness that 'sells' this mildly pleasurable activity to us.

Tips & Tools
From apathy to flow
Have you ever wondered how much your TV time affects your ability to immerse yourself in other rewarding activities? Try turning your TV on no more than three times per week. Once your show has finished, switch the TV off, don't channel-surf. Be mindful of the choices you are making – select the programmes you want to watch at the start of the week and stick to them.

In addition to autotelic activities, Csikszentmihalyi (1997) talks of *autotelic personality* – a person who 'generally does things for their own sake rather than in order to achieve some later external goal' (p. 117). These people develop skills that help them get into the flow state frequently, skills that include curiosity, interest in life, persistence and low self-centredness.[3]

Tips & Tools
Finding flow
Identify activities that help you to get into flow (activities that you might call 'serious play'). Gradually increase the difficulty or complexity of these activities, ensuring they match your growing skills. If an activity is too easy, make it more challenging. On the other hand, if it's too hard, find a way to boost your skill level.

Dangers of flow

With flow having become such a popular notion and a desirable state, few pause to ask whether it is always good. In fact, the activities in which flow is found can be morally good or bad. Gambling, for example – especially games like bridge or poker – has all the conditions necessary for flow: the games are challenging and require a high level of skill to stand any chance of winning.

Even activities that are morally good or neutral, like mountain climbing, chess or PlayStation, can become addictive, so much so that life without them can feel static, boring and meaningless. A simple non-gambling game on your computer, like solitaire, which many people use to 'switch off' for a few minutes, can take over your life. This happens when, instead of being a choice, a flow-inducing activity becomes a necessity.

Csikszentmihalyi himself is very much aware of the dangers of flow. He writes (1992: 62):

> enjoyable activities that produce flow have a potentially negative effect: while they are capable of improving the quality of existence by creating order in the mind, they can become addictive, at which point the self becomes captive of a certain kind of order, and is then unwilling to cope with the ambiguities of life.

Addiction to flow can also lead to losing a larger perspective. A workaholic manager may lose himself in flow at work until 10 or 11 at night, forgetting dinner, his family or saying goodnight to the children.

Csikszentmihalyi (1992: 70) also adds:

> The flow experience, like everything else, is not 'good' in an absolute sense. It is good only in that it has the potential to make life more rich, intense, and meaningful; it is good because it increases the strengths and complexity of the self. But whether the consequence of any particular instance of flow is good in a larger sense needs to be discussed and evaluated in terms of more inclusive social criteria.

The issue regarding flow is not only how we can make it happen, but also how we can manage it: using it to enhance life, yet being able to let go when necessary.

Other optimal experiences

Flow is not the only optimal experience. A humanistic psychologist, Abraham Maslow (1908–1970), coined the term *peak experience* to describe intensely joyous and exciting moments in the lives of every individual. In these moments, we feel more whole, integrated, aware of ourselves and deeply happy. We have a sense of transcendence, awe, unity and meaningfulness in life. Often these experiences have a spiritual quality about them. The peak moments are often inspired by intense occurrences – moments of love, exposure to great art or music, the overwhelming beauty of nature, or even tragic events. Maslow, like Csikszentmihalyi with regard to flow, believed that all individuals are capable of peak experiences, but those who achieve self-actualization are more likely to have them. Although many characteristics are shared (e.g. absorption, spontaneity, loss of time), peak experience differs from flow in the presence (rather than loss) of the sense of self, the rarity of its occurrence and having almost a mystical quality about it (Privette, 1983). While flow experiences are encouraged, Maslow cautioned against seeking peak experiences for their own sake.

We have a long way to go in learning about the optimal states of human existence. Little is known about *microflow* activities (such as doodling), *shared*, rather than individualized, flow, in which the whole is greater than the sum of its parts (like in a musical jam session) or a *plateau experience* (which is a continuous peak experience). Positive psychology might potentially be a vehicle for exploring the complexity of these and other positive human experiences.

Notes

1 If you want to play a spelling challenge with yourself, write down the surname Csikszentmihalyi, look at it for 10 seconds, place a piece of paper over it and try writing it down. See how many mistakes you have made, and then repeat the exercise.
2 See, for example, Butler-Bowdon, T. (2003). *50 Self-help Classics*. London and Yarmouth: Nicholas Brealey Publishing.
3 See pp. 65–66 for more on doing things for their own sake, or intrinsic motivation.

Further reading

Csikszentmihalyi, M. (2007). *Finding flow*. New York: Basic Books.
Privette, G. (1983). Peak experience, peak performance, and peak flow: A comparative analysis of positive human experiences. *Journal of Personality and Social Psychology*, 45, 1369–1379.

Chapter Five
Happiness and Subjective Well-being

History of happiness

Happiness has been a topic of interest for many centuries, starting with ancient Greek philosophy, through post-Enlightenment Western-European moral philosophy (especially Utilitarianism) to current quality-of-life and well-being research in social, political and economic sciences (Veenhoven, 1991a). Today, happiness as a concept seems to be readily embraced by most people and appears to be more valued than the pursuit of money, moral goodness or going to heaven (King & Napa, 1998). Not surprisingly, during the past thirty years and especially since the creation of positive psychology, psychology too has turned its attention towards the study of happiness and well-being.

There are several reasons why the field of well-being is flourishing at the moment:

- First, Western countries have achieved a sufficient level of affluence, so that survival is no longer a central factor in people's lives. Quality of life is becoming more important than matters of economic prosperity.
- Personal happiness is becoming more important because of growing trends towards individualism.
- Finally, a number of valid and reliable measures have been developed, which have allowed the study of well-being to establish itself as a serious and recognized discipline (Diener et al., 2001).

Who is happy?

The answer is simple but a little unexpected – almost everyone. The collated results of 916 surveys of 1.1 million people in 45 nations show that, on a scale of 0 to 10, the average score was 6.75. So, people are generally more happy than they are unhappy (Myers, 2000). Between 84 and 89 per cent of Americans, for example, score themselves above neutral in happiness inventories. Most countries are well above the neutral point, the exception being the former Soviet bloc countries (e.g. Bulgaria, Russia, Belarus, Latvia), where the average is somewhere close to 5 on a 10-point scale (Argyle, 2001).

Who is not happy?

The same groups usually have the lowest happiness ratings, including: those who have recently lost their partners, clients new to therapy, hospitalized alcoholics, new inmates and students under political repression.

Why is it good to be happy?

The common-sense answer to this question is that happiness is good because it feels good. However, research evidence demonstrates that there are other benefits too: positive affect and well-being lead to sociability, better health, success, self-regulation and helping behaviour.

Interestingly, well-being enhances creativity and divergent thinking. It appears that happiness, similar to positive affect, stimulates playing with new ideas. New research has also shown that happy people persist longer at a task that is not very enjoyable in itself (tell your boss that only the happiest employees should be attending boring meetings!), are better at multi-tasking and are more systematic and attentive (Diener, 2001). When it comes to health, happiness is known to have a beneficial effect on immune system functioning – experimental studies demonstrate that it even protects us from the common cold (Cohen et al., 2003)!

What is even more fascinating is that well-being is associated with longevity. One study analysed the application letters of nuns entering convents at the age of 18 for expressions of happiness. It is important to note that all of these nuns had a very similar, moderate lifestyle – they didn't smoke or drink, had a balanced diet and worked as teachers. The results indicated that happiness expressed in these letters at the age of 18 predicted life duration. Years later, at the age of 85, 90 per cent of nuns whose happiness was in the upper quarter were still alive, compared with 34 per cent of those who were least happy. Even at the age of 94, over half (54 per cent) of the happiest nuns were still alive, while only 11 per cent of those whose happiness fell into the lowest quarter were still living. So it looks like happiness can buy you an extra 9.4 years of life (Danner et al., 2001)!

Before we go any further . . .

Would you like to test yourself once again? If your answer is yes, follow the instructions below.

In the box below, you will find five statements with which you may agree or disagree. Using the scale of 1–7 provided, indicate your agreement with each statement by placing the appropriate number on the line following that statement. Try to be open and honest in your responding.

The 7-point scale

1	2	3	4	5	6	7
strongly disagree	disagree	slightly disagree	neither agree nor disagree	slightly agree	agree	strongly agree

In most ways my life is close to my ideal —
The conditions of my life are excellent —
I am satisfied with my life —
So far I have got the important things I want in life —
If I could live my life over, I would change almost nothing —

Now add together all five numbers to get your overall score. It should be between 5 and 35. The results of this questionnaire can show how satisfied you are with your life (Diener et al., 1985). An answer in the region of 15 to 25 is considered average, below 14 indicates that your life satisfaction is less than average, while if your total score falls between 26 and 35 you are probably quite happy with your life.

Read on to find out more about life satisfaction and the part it plays in our happiness.

What happiness really is, or the science of subjective well-being

There is a big debate in psychology about whether happiness can and should be measured objectively or subjectively. Some argue that it cannot possibly be measured objectively because none of the obvious behaviours can be linked to happiness in a reliable manner. Even an outgoing and friendly appearance, which is seen frequently among happy people, can be used as a mask by those who are unhappy. Others, however, including Nobel Prize winner Daniel Kahneman, believe in the objective assessment of happiness, which could be gathered from averaged out multiple assessments of people's moods over a period of time. This way, a happiness assessment would not need to be tied to memory and retrospective accounts (Kahneman, 1999). Nevertheless, the subjective paradigm appears to prevail at the moment, and this is what I will focus on here.

So far in this chapter, I have been using the words 'happiness' and 'well-being' interchangeably. This is because the notion of *subjective well-being* (SWB) is used in research literature as a substitute for the term 'happiness'. It encompasses how people evaluate their own lives in terms of *cognitive* and *affective* explanations, and can be represented in the following way (Diener, 2000):

SWB = SATISFACTION WITH LIFE + AFFECT

The first, cognitive part of subjective well-being is expressed by *life satisfaction*. Life satisfaction represents one's assessment of one's own life. One is satisfied when there is little or no discrepancy between the present and what is thought to be an ideal or deserved situation. On the other hand, dissatisfaction is a result of a substantial discrepancy between present conditions and the ideal standard. Dissatisfaction can also be a result of comparing oneself with others. *Affect* represents the emotional side of SWB. The notion of affect (which was discussed in Chapter 2) comprises both positive and negative moods and emotions that are associated with our everyday experiences.

Even though common sense would suggest that we should feel most happy if we experience the maximum amount of intense positive affect and not very frequent negative affect, research demonstrates that this is not the case. The research shows that, while it is very important to experience positive affect often, intense positive affect is not necessary for well-being. It appears that intense positive emotions usually come at a price, as they are often followed by periods of low affect. Also, they can negatively affect the evaluation of subsequent (usually less intense) positive experiences (Diener et al., 1991).

Back to practical matters – can we raise our subjective well-being?

A number of theories say that it is impossible to permanently change someone's level of happiness. One of these theories, the so-called *Zero-sum*, says that happiness is cyclical and that happy and unhappy periods follow each other. Any attempt to increase happiness will soon be nullified by a consequent unhappy period. Another theory claims that happiness is a fixed characteristic and is, therefore, not open to change, although happiness is not quite as stable during adolescence and early adulthood and can be affected by major life changes. Therefore, it is more likely that happiness 'tends to get' fixed, rather than being fixed from the very beginning (Veenhoven, 1991a).

Adaptation theory predicts that although happiness reacts to negative and positive life events, it returns to baseline shortly afterwards. Lottery winners soon revert to their normal level of well-being, and paraplegics and quadriplegics seem to adjust to their conditions and revert almost to their previous level of well-being (Brickman et al., 1978). This is called the 'hedonic treadmill'. It has been discovered that only life events that occurred during the previous two or three months influence well-being (Suh et al., 1996). However, despite the evidence that people get adjusted to both lottery winning and spinal injuries, there are certain conditions (such as widowhood and long-term unemployment) to which people never adjust completely (Seligman, 2002).

Taking into account the findings of many scholars, Seligman offers the happiness formula: H = S + C + V, where H stands for happiness, S for a set range, C for the circumstances and V for the factors under voluntary control. S is a genetically determined level of happiness, which remains relatively stable throughout the lifespan and returns to its original level soon after the majority of significant life events. It determines happiness up to about 50 per cent. C is the circumstances we've already considered (and accounts for about 10 per cent). So, if you want to be happy, get married, join a church but don't bother about making more money, staying healthy, getting educated or moving to a sunnier climate. Finally, factors under voluntary control (V) refer to intentional and effortful practices a person can choose to engage in (which account for about 40 per cent) (Seligman, 2002). Of course, this formula is far from perfect. Genes and marriage are hardly the same fruit, and are more like apples and pears that cannot be added up. Nevertheless, the formula gives an indication of possibility and the room to manoeuvre (the 40 per cent).

What is important for happiness and what is not?

Which of the following would you say are important for happiness: money, friends, having children, getting married, looks, health, moving to a better climate? Is your age important? What about your level of education? The safety of your community? Common sense predicts that the most likely source of satisfaction with life is objective circumstances, but often this is not the case. There is a weak relationship between happiness and many life circumstances we consider so important that we would sacrifice years of our lives to have them. Compare your thoughts with Table 5.1, which summarizes the research findings on the correlates[1] of happiness, and see whether you've got it right (Argyle, 2001).

A word of warning here – unravelling cause and effect is not easy. Although these correlates are often considered to be the causes of happiness, they may as well be its consequences. For example, it may be that having good friends brings happiness or that those who are happy attract good friends.

TABLE 5.1 THE TRUTH AS RESEARCH KNOWS IT

SWB IS RELATED TO:	SWB IS NOT REALLY RELATED TO:
Optimism	Age (although there are somewhat contradictory findings in this respect)
Extraversion	Physical attractiveness
Social connections, i.e. close friendships	Money (once the basic needs are met, the difference between the very rich and alright is small)
Being married (marriage still scores better than cohabitation, although the latter is picking up as a predictor of SWB in individualistic societies)	Gender (women are more often depressed but also more often joyful)
Having engaging work	Educational level
Religion or spirituality	Having children (see the next section for further clarification)
Leisure	Moving to a sunnier climate (in fact, moving to Australia will increase your SWB only by 1–2 per cent)
Good sleep and exercise	Crime prevention
Social class (through lifestyle differences and better coping methods)	Housing
Subjective health (what you think about your health)	Objective health (what doctors say)

Happiness and personality

A meta-analysis of 148 studies by DeNeve and Cooper found that, of 137 personality characteristics that had been studied (as of 1996), the following were moderately predictive of happiness: trust, emotional stability, locus of control (what happens to me is the result of my effort rather than luck, chance or fate), desire for control, hardiness (feelings of control, commitment and challenge), absence of tension, self-esteem, absence of neuroticism (undue anxiety), extraversion (being outgoing), agreeableness (easy to get along with), and repressiveness-defensiveness in the face of life difficulties. Some of the above personality characteristics are probably easier to change than others, and as a result are more or less likely candidates for helping to increase happiness (e.g. changing your level of extraversion is actually quite difficult).

Happiness and relationships

One of the strongest predictors (and not only correlates!) of happiness is social relationships. In fact, to be happy we need to spend six to seven hours a day in social settings, and up to nine if our jobs are stressful (Rath & Harter, 2010). This applies regardless of whether we are extraverted or introverted (Froh et al., 2007). In their study of exceptionally happy people (10 per cent of 222 college students), Diener and Seligman (2002) found only one main difference between the happiest and the rest of the students. The very happy people had a rich and fulfilling social life. They spent the least time alone, had good relationships with friends and had a current romantic partner. They did not have fewer negative and more positive events, nor differed on amount of sleep, TV watching, exercise, smoking, drinking, etc. Perhaps not surprisingly, frequency of sexual intercourse is strongly associated with happiness.

Marriage usually leads to a rapid increase in SWB, which, unfortunately, comes down after a while. However, it does not return to the starting point, but stays at a higher level than before marriage. So marriage changes the set point of SWB, although this change is not large. However, if your relationship is on the rocks, you are likely to be less happy than people who are unmarried or divorced.

Interesting facts about well-being

- Real income has risen dramatically in the prosperous nations over the last 50 years, but levels of SWB have remained flat (Easterlin et al., 2010).
- People in wealthy nations appear to be much happier than in poorer ones but this finding does not hold true for some nations (e.g. Brazil) (Diener et al., 1995).
- Denmark and Costa Rica keep competing for the title of the happiest country on Earth (Hefferon & Boniwell, 2011).
- Desiring wealth leaves one less happy (Kasser, 2002).
- Making an extra $10,000 per year would increase your happiness only by about 2 per cent (Christakis & Fowler, 2009).
- Spending money on others increases your happiness (Dunn et al., 2008).
- People who go to church are happier and live longer, although this may be explained by the social support that belonging to a religious community gives to people (Ciarrocchi et al., 2008).
- Having children does not make you happier and having under-fives and teenagers actually makes you less happy. Saying that, having children can make your life more meaningful, and also parents tend to live longer (Kobrin & Hendershot, 1977).
- Children genetically predisposed to unhappiness can benefit from early positive environmental influences better than their more genetically contented peers (Belsky & Pluess, 2008).
- Hanging out with happy people will increase your level of happiness (Christakis & Fowler, 2009).

- Watching soap operas enhances well-being (Argyle, 2001).
- All objective life circumstances combined account for no more than 10 per cent of variance in well-being (Diener, 1999; Ryan & Deci, 2001).

Note

1 Correlates are associations between any two things. For example, height in children correlates with age (i.e. taller children are likely to be older).

Further reading

Christakis, N., & Fowler, J. (2009). *Connected: The surprising power of our social networks and how they shape our lives*. New York: Little, Brown.
Diener, E., & Biswas-Diener, R. (2008). *Happiness: Unlocking the mysteries of psychological wealth*. Malden, MA: Wiley/Blackwell.

Great ! I can affect 40 per cent of my happiness but what do I do? (Carr, 2004; Myers, 1992; Seligman, 2002; Sheldon & Lyubomirsky, 2004)

Chapter Six

Is Happiness Necessary or Sufficient? The Concept of Eudaimonic Well-being

Problems with existing approaches to happiness

Is happiness enough for a good life? This question is becoming increasingly prominent in positive psychology. Is feeling good an adequate measure of someone's quality of life? Do we really know what it means to *be subjectively well* when we assess someone's subjective well-being? Many researchers believe we don't, saying that the current definition of well-being came about almost accidentally. First, researchers developed well-being questionnaires (because they needed to evaluate various interventions), then they derived the definition of well-being from these questionnaires, without paying much attention to whether they actually captured the richness of human wellness and happiness (Ryff & Keyes, 1995).

It is probably true to say that contemporary literature on well-being largely ignores the contributions of humanistic and existential thinkers like Maslow, Rogers, Jung and Allport (McGregor & Little, 1998). It also doesn't pay much attention to the complexity of philosophical conceptions of happiness, even though philosophy dealt with this subject long before psychology existed.

Can someone be truly fulfilled without knowing what he or she is living for, what the point is, the meaning of one's existence? Is it possible to be truly well without moving a finger to change something in oneself, without growing and developing as a person? This is what is missing from the current mainstream theories of well-being – the notions of growth, self-actualization and meaning.

The current theories of well-being seem to give a rather bare, one-sided picture of well-being. In fact, what they do seem to cover quite well is the notion of hedonism – striving for maximization of pleasure (positive affect) and minimization of pain (negative affect). This hedonic view can be traced to Aristippus, a Greek philosopher who believed that the goal of life is to experience maximum pleasure, and later to Utilitarian philosophers (Ryan & Deci, 2001).

An alternative to hedonic happiness

Recently, another approach to a good life has arisen out of the historical and philosophical debris – the idea of *eudaimonic well-being*. Aristotle was the originator of the concept of eudaimonia (from *daimon* = true nature). He deemed happiness to be a vulgar idea, stressing that not all desires are worth pursuing because, even though some of them may yield pleasure, they do not produce wellness. Aristotle thought that true happiness is achieved by leading a virtuous life and doing what is worth doing. He argued that realizing human potential is the ultimate human goal. This idea was further developed in history by prominent thinkers such as Stoics, who stressed the value of self-discipline, and John Locke, who argued that happiness is pursued through prudence.

Humanistic psychology and the actualizing tendency

Humanistic psychologists, such as Maslow (famous for developing the hierarchy of needs) and Rogers, were probably the first 'eudaimonists' in the twentieth century. Humanistic psychology grew up in the 1960s out of the climate of pessimistic psychoanalysis and behaviourism that reduced humans to machines responding to stimuli. The premise of humanistic psychology was that people have a free will and make choices that influence their well-being. What also makes it very different from other perspectives in psychology is belief in the *actualizing tendency* – a

fundamental motivation towards growth. Rogers (1961: 351), the originator of the concept, describes it as:

> man's tendency to actualize himself, to become potentialities. By
> this I mean the directional trend which is evident in all organic and
> human life – the urge to expand, develop, mature – the tendency to
> express and activate all the capacities of the organism and the self.
> This tendency may become deeply buried under layer after layer of
> encrusted psychological defences; it may be hidden behind elabo-
> rate facades that deny its existence; it is my belief, however, based
> on my experience, that it exists in every individual, and awaits only
> the proper conditions to be released and expressed.

What lives under the umbrella of eudaimonia?

So, if you agree with the claim that just feeling good is not good enough
for a good life, you are in good company. There are several theories of
well-being that try to co-exist under a relatively broad concept of eudaimonia. I'll discuss a few of these in this chapter.

Tips & Tools
Daimon in action
Daimon refers to potentialities of each person, realization of which
leads to the greatest fulfilment. Efforts to live in accordance with one's
daimon, the congruence between this and people's life activities, lead
to the experience of eudaimonia (Waterman, 1993).

Psychological well-being

If you think you've just about managed to grasp the difference between
subjective well-being (SWB) and satisfaction with life (SWL), I bet

you are going to be delighted to see me throwing something called PWB into the discussion pot.

PWB stands for *psychological well-being*, which is a model of well-being widely advocated by a psychology professor, Carol Ryff (Ryff & Keyes, 1995; Ryff & Singer, 1998; Ryff et al., 2004). I wouldn't be surprised if she used the word 'psychological' only because subjective was already taken. Ryff analysed many various approaches to happiness in different sub-fields of psychology and came to the conclusion that well-being should be seen as consisting of six components. These components are: *self-acceptance* (positive evaluation of oneself and one's life), *personal growth, purpose in life, positive relations with others, environmental mastery* (the capacity to effectively manage one's life and the surrounding environment) and *autonomy*.

This model is quite a lot broader than what is on offer in the hedonic camp, but is it right? Ryff has run many studies providing so-called empirical support for her model. A lot of other people have run many studies

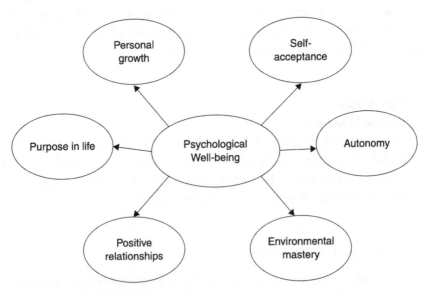

Ryff's model of psychological well-being

that haven't:[1] they found that all six components can be accounted for by only two dimensions, one corresponding to hedonic and the other to eudaimonic well-being (McGregor & Little, 1998; Vittersø, undated).

While all the components of PWB seem important, they still appear somewhat arbitrary. Would the model really suffer if one or two of the elements were not there? Would it be enriched if something else, like inner harmony, were to be added?

Self-determination theory

Another eudaimonic model, the self-determination theory (SDT) developed by Ryan and Deci, postulates the existence of three inherent fundamental needs, which are universal (found throughout different cultures and times). These basic psychological nutrients are:

- *Autonomy* – the need to choose what one is doing, being an agent of one's own life.
- *Competence* – the need to feel confident in doing what one is doing.
- *Relatedness* – the need to have human connections that are close and secure, while still respecting autonomy and facilitating competence.

SDT asserts that when these needs are satisfied, motivation and well-being are enhanced, and when they are limited, there is a negative impact on our well-functioning (Ryan & Deci, 2000). Quite a number of psychologists agree that these three needs are the most basic ones, although self-esteem is also frequently mentioned. Ryan and Deci see a big difference between PWB and SDT in that autonomy, competence and relatedness foster well-being in their model, whereas Ryff uses these concepts to define it.

Other eudaimonic theories

Csikszentmihalyi's concept of *autotelic* personality is also claiming its place under the eudaimonic happiness umbrella. Autotelic people (see

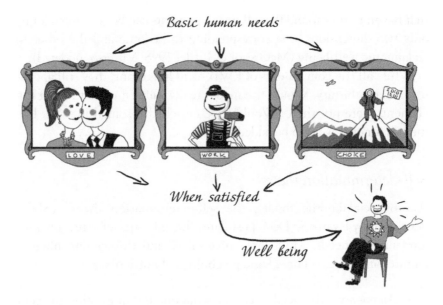

Chapter 4) are those who often engage in activities for their own sake, and experience flow states frequently. One problem with allocating flow into the eudaimonic camp is that some of Csikszentmihalyi's characteristics of flow, including losing track of time and forgetting personal problems, seem to have much more to do with hedonic enjoyment than with eudaimonic endeavours.

In the early 2000s, Waterman proposed a description of eudaimonia that he called *personal expressiveness* (Waterman et al., 2003; Waterman, 2008). For him, eudaimonia is experienced through engagement in activities that make one feel alive, that express who one really is, that one is intensely involved in, that one feels one was meant to do, that make one particularly complete or fulfilled, and that one has a special fit or meshing with. Interestingly, for this researcher eudaimonia does not exclude hedonic happiness – Waterman shows that personal expressiveness tends to be accompanied by feelings of hedonic enjoyment. On the other hand, hedonic enjoyment is not necessarily accompanied by personal expressiveness. Given that Waterman's description of personal expressiveness is not that far removed from that of flow, the finding of a merger between eudaimonia and hedonic enjoyment helps to account for the criticisms of flow as a form of eudaimonia raised above.

The person behind the positive psychology movement, Martin Seligman (2002), introduced an *authentic happiness* model, in which he distinguishes between the pleasant life, the good life and the meaningful life in an attempt to work out what well-being really is. The pleasant life is devoted to pursuit of *positive emotions*, and can be paralleled with hedonic well-being. In the good life, one would use one's dominant character strengths to obtain *engagement*, a complete immersion in an activity, akin to flow. Finally, *meaningful* life is about using your strengths in the service of something greater than yourself. In 2011, the authentic happiness model got upgraded to a well-being model, consisting of the same three elements plus an extra two – *accomplishment* (the pursuit of achievement, success and winning for their own sake) and *relationships* (connecting with other people). The first letters of all the five components result in *PERMA*, which is how Seligman's new theory of well-being is usually referred to (Seligman, 2011). Seligman believes that both pursuits of engagement/flow and meaning can be considered eudaimonic.[2] The research of Seligman and his colleagues shows that when people engage in hedonic activities (e.g. leisure, rest or fun), they experience many pleasant feelings, are more energetic and have low negative affect. In fact, during these activities, they are happier than those who engage in eudaimonic pursuits. In the long run, however, those who lead a more eudaimonic existence (work on developing their potentials and skills, learning something) are more satisfied with their lives (Huta et al., 2003).

Vitters∅ and colleagues have proposed a *functional well-being model* in which eudaimonia signals and promotes change and growth, and motivates behaviour in challenging environments, while hedonia signals and regulates stability, equilibrium and return to homeostasis. In fact, this is the difference between being in the process of achieving (eudaimonia) and having arrived or achieved, whether this relates to needs, goals or conceptual understanding (hedonia). These authors also talk about stable hedonic and eudaimonic orientations, implying that some of us have more hedonic or more eudaimonic personalities. Vittersø discusses possible neurological mechanisms underlying these orientations: the dopamine system that underlies interest and novelty-seeking may support eudaimonia, while the endogenous opioid system that underlies pleasure and regulation of homeostatic processes may, in fact, support hedonia (Vittersø et al., 2010).

The further one delves into the area, the more variety one discovers when it comes to defining what eudaimonic well-being is. Some researchers claim that eudaimonic well-being is best achieved through personal development and growth (Compton et al., 1996), others

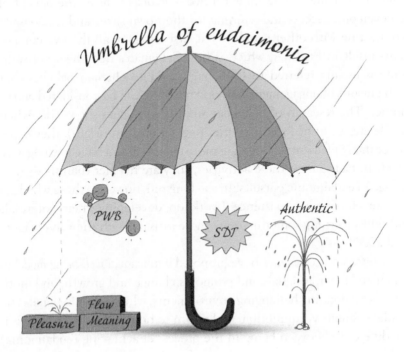

Oops ... we have a problem

through finding meaning in one's life (King & Napa, 1998; McGregor & Little, 1998). One way or another, they all agree that there must be something else out there in addition to pure pleasure and happiness, although the umbrella of eudaimonic well-being grows larger and larger year after year . . .

I wonder if you noticed a little problem with eudaimonic well-being? It's a MESS! Eudaimonic well-being is not just an umbrella concept for many vaguely related theories; it's a pot in which anything that is not related to pleasure is mixed up.

So let's take a look inside this pot once again. Some authors define eudaimonia as actualization of human potential (Waterman, 1993), while others associate it with frequent experiences of flow states (Csikszentmihalyi, 1992). Other commonly used definitions include: realizing one's true nature/true self (Vittersø, 2003), personal growth, meaning, and the totality of the six components of Ryff's psychological well-being (Ryff & Keyes, 1995). Seligman defines eudaimonia as both flow and meaning. Can somebody please tell me what eudaimonic well-being actually is?

Despite their attempts to shed light on the construct of well-being, eudaimonic definitions often make the picture even more complicated. Is realizing your true nature the same as personal development? And what if your true nature is calling you to violence? Is growth the same as meaning? Carol Ryff is probably right to distinguish between the two. Meaning may well be found in personal growth, yet it can also be found in serving others or in believing in God, which means that these two should not be identified. Are positive relationships important for eudaimonic well-being? Perhaps, but they also seem to be pretty important for happiness or hedonic well-being (see Chapter 5). Do people really experience eudaimonic well-being differently from hedonic well-being? Critics of the movement say that if the feeling is the same, the differences between 'two kinds of happiness' are overblown (Kashdan et al., 2008). Supporters of the distinction, on the other hand, try to identify distinct emotions and feelings associated with eudaimonia, such as interest, engagement and peak experiences. Finally, if eudaimonia and hedonia are indeed distinct forms of happiness, we would expect to find different patterns of predictor and outcome variables – that is, what leads to eudaimonia and what comes out of it? Early research shows that, unlike hedonic well-being, one's level of education is associated with eudaimonia (i.e. the more, the better) (Boniwell & Osin, in prep.). Furthermore, it may be the case, for example, that people with high eudaimonic well-being can find greater fulfilment in working or recover more quickly from a traumatic event (Huta, in press).

On the basis of these somewhat contradictory theories and my own research, I would like to suggest that eudaimonic well-being can be achieved by pursuing either of the following two routes – personal development or transcendence (Boniwell & Osin, in prep.). So don't give up yet, it all might make sense in the end!

Personal development

Personal development is related to striving for change, striving to understand oneself and the world better, striving to grow as a person, to become better in one's chosen fields and domains of life. The routes of personal development lie in the actualizing tendency, yet the tendency on its own is not enough. Development is often an effortful process, involving overcoming challenges and barriers, which can be external or internal.

Growth and personal life changes are not always experienced as pleasant (Maslow, 1968). Researchers have found that even positive subjective changes can decrease positive affect (Keyes et al., 2002). For example, one study established that therapy clients who perceived more improvement in their functioning reported more depressive symptoms and lower levels of self-acceptance, but more personal growth at the same time. This is because any change is associated with loss, even if what is lost is an unproductive or even negative pattern. Carl Rogers, one of the fathers of humanistic psychology, observed that people who made real progress towards what can be considered 'a good life' would typically not regard themselves as happy or content. He writes: 'The good life is a *process*, not a state of being' (1961: 186). Note the similarity of this statement to Vittersø's functional model of well-being.

Tips & Tools
Personal development workout

To clarify your direction, imagine yourself in 10 or 20 years' time and consider what sort of person you would like to be then, and how it can be achieved (Popovic, 2005).

When psychologists try to measure development, they often look to what extent individuals are open to experiences or to what extent they are interested in learning (Vittersø, undated). Yet, if we apply common sense, it becomes quite clear that openness to experience is needed not only to grow but also to experience pleasure, which is a facet of hedonic well-being. While *interest in learning* is a very important aspect, it can hardly be the only indicator of human development. So how do we know whether the process of development is taking place, whether we are actually growing?

Research suggests that attributes of responsibility and commitment to challenge are important aspects of a eudaimonic personality (Boniwell & Osin, in prep.). *Responsibility* relates not only to oneself and one's own actions, but also to taking care of others, the environment and the world at large. *Commitment to challenge*, on the other hand, is about drawing satisfaction from something that stretches and develops one's abilities – the antithesis to an effortless life!

Several factors help us to excel in our development, including delayed gratification, grit and emotional control. People high in *delayed gratification* find it easy to postpone immediate pleasures in favour of pursuing important goals, such as completing work, for example.

The value of delayed gratification is reflected in one of the most famous psychology studies, referred to as the Stanford marshmallow experiment. Conducted in 1972 by Walter Mischel, the experiment presented pre-school children with a choice of either eating a marshmallow immediately or waiting for fifteen minutes and getting two marshmallows instead. Longitudinal research revealed that those able to resist temptation were significantly more competent as adolescents and scored higher academically many years later (Shoda et al., 1990). What is even more astonishing, however, is the fact that these advantages remained forty years later – a 2011 study found that children better at delaying gratification carried this competence to adulthood, also showing consistent differences in certain areas of the brain linked to addictive behaviours (Casey et al., 2011). *Grit*, or the capacity to sustain effort and keep working even in the face of obstacles, has recently been found to be more important than IQ in predicting academic achievement and long-term success (Duckworth et al., 2007). Finally, *emotional control*, or the ability to manage impulses and emotions, is another essential skill underlying personal development.

Transcendence

Transcendence is related to dedication and commitment to something or somebody other than oneself. It is about finding purpose in one's life and acting in accordance with this purpose. However, this purpose is necessarily related to transcending the personal (without losing oneself) for the sake of something larger than oneself (it can be children, meaningful work, the wider community, or a spiritual pathway) and then taking action to contribute to something larger than oneself. Transcendence thus leads to some external utility of one's life, through objective life results or virtuous living (Veenhoven, 2000).

Transcendence is a eudaimonic pathway to well-being that is distinct from personal development (although undoubtedly the two can co-exist). For example, a mother who dedicates her life to raising (rather than merely looking after) her children as fully functioning human beings may not have much time to devote to her own personal development, at least until the children leave home.

Transcendence is sometimes (though this is not a daily occurrence) accompanied by so-called peak experiences, which are moments of intense beauty, of feeling one with the universe or mystical experiences (see Chapter 4).

Many scholars, including Aristotle, Ryff, Seligman, McGregor and Little, speak about meaning, purpose, transcending oneself for the sake of the greater good. I hope that introducing this common term will allow for greater integration between theories.

The very last note . . .

There is one more caveat to the story of hedonic and eudaimonic well-being. You may remember from the previous chapter the concept of satisfaction with life. It has been firmly allocated into the hedonic camp by many proponents of the eudaimonic paradigm, but it is actually questionable whether this needs to be the case. One can be satisfied with one's life if one wants to pursue happiness and is pursuing happiness successfully, OR if one chooses to live a more eudaimonically oriented life and this is exactly what one is doing. Remember, life satisfaction is nothing more than congruence between the present and an ideal situation, both of which are a reflection of the person's own subjective appreciation of life (Diener, 1984). Therefore, life satisfaction can be conceived of as an independent, subjective evaluation of the current status of one's life, which can be either hedonically or eudaimonically oriented.

Notes

1 You have probably guessed by now that empirical support and research evidence are not necessarily set in stone.
2 See above regarding potential problems with flow as a eudaimonic pursuit.

Further reading

David, S., Boniwell, I., & Conley, A. (2012). *Oxford handbook of happiness.* Oxford: Oxford University Press.

Chapter Seven
Meaning in Making: Values, Motivation and Life Goals

Now that we know what makes us truly fulfilled, let's consider what else can help us get there. This chapter deals with three interrelated topics – values, motivation and life goals, all of which play a role in enhancing hedonic and eudaimonic well-being. Even though it is important that our fundamental biological (safety, hunger, thirst) and psychological (autonomy, relatedness, competence) needs are satisfied, this is not sufficient for optimal functioning. To make reasoned choices and to act, we need to know what our values and beliefs are. We need to be motivated to start doing the things that we choose to do. Finally, we need to set goals that are achievable, relevant to us and reflect our deeply held values.

Values

Values are the things that are important to us. They are deeply held beliefs that we usually internalize during our upbringing or decide on as we grow older. It is essential to distinguish *needs* from values. Needs are inborn, they exist even if we are not aware of them and are universal. Values, on the other hand, are learnt or chosen, are parts of our consciousness and are specific to each of us. Needs are pretty stable – we want to eat today and we'll want to eat tomorrow (or even later today). Values are open to change. Few people can maintain absolutely identical values throughout their lifetimes.

Values form the basis of why we do what we do. For instance, they help us to harness and prioritize needs. If we valued everything equally, we wouldn't be able to act, because we wouldn't know where to start (Locke, 2002). Values are especially useful in explaining why we do things that we don't actually like doing. Not many people enjoy changing nappies, yet the value of caring overrides the value of what we like or dislike in the vast majority of cases (otherwise there would be many more frustrated babies out there).

Modern society no longer offers us a reliable and convincing set of values. In fact, we are in a so-called 'value-gap' with regard to the loss of consensus (Baumeister & Vohs, 2002). We have learnt to realize and accept that other people's values can be different from our own, and with that our own values became, to some extent, arbitrary.

Losing values, or not knowing which values to choose, can be devastating. Countries in the former Soviet bloc, for example, have undergone an astonishing experience, in that the values that people held were shattered over a very short period of time, with nothing to replace them.

Shalom Schwartz identified ten values that he believes can be universal (found cross-culturally): *power, achievement, hedonism, stimulation, self-direction, universalism, benevolence, tradition, conformity* and *security* (Schwartz, 1994). Indeed, research offers a lot of support for his claim that the list is comprehensive.[1] If you had to guess, which of the above values do you think are associated with subjective well-being? Self-direction and achievement values (probably because they emphasize autonomy and competence) appear to be, while tradition and conformity values are related to lower well-being. This is because they rely on so-called extrinsic motivation (which will be discussed in the next section of the chapter).

Values are often linked to worries. If you think that worries are something to do with mental health and nothing to do with positive psychology, think again. Researchers distinguish between two types of worries – micro worries and macro worries (Boehnke et al., 1998). *Micro worries* are all about yourself and others close to you ('Will I get an interview?', 'What if he leaves me?'). Not surprisingly, they lead to poor well-being. Moreover, people who have a lot of these worries usually hold power and hedonism values. *Macro worries*, on the other hand, are about society, the world or universal issues (AIDS in Africa or presidential elections in the USA). People who are high on universalism and benevolence values have these types of worries, together with a higher level of well-being (Schwartz et al., 2000). So, worrying is actually good for you, as long as it is not self-centred.

Motivation

Why do you get up in the morning? Why don't you just stay in bed all day doing nothing? Motivation is the force behind getting up, going to work, opening a study book in the middle of the night, etc. Yet this force is not as simple as it looks on the surface.

There are two fundamental types of motivation: intrinsic and extrinsic. *Intrinsic* motivation reflects the inborn human tendency to seek out novelty and challenges, to explore the world, to exercise our capacities. When we are intrinsically motivated, we do something for the sake of it, simply out of enjoyment or interest. We are *extrinsically* motivated when we do an activity for the sake of something else or to attain some other outcome (e.g. going to work to earn money).

> **Tips & Tools**
> **Awakening intrinsic motivation**
> Intrinsic motivation is enhanced for activities that are moderately challenging, those we feel we can do well, or that give us satisfaction (Bandura, 1997).

Self-determination theory, which we touched upon in the preceding chapter, proposes four different subtypes of extrinsic motivation: external, introjected, identified and integrated (Ryan & Deci, 2000).

- *External* motivation occurs when we feel driven by outside forces, performing an activity either to obtain a reward or to avoid punishment. We do something because we *have to* do it.
- *Introjected* motivation is based on self-control, acting in order to avoid guilt, pressure and anxiety. We do something because we would feel guilty if we didn't.
- *Identified* motivation means we do something because we can see why it is important (even though we don't enjoy it).
- Finally, *integrated* motivation means we do something because we fully subscribe to the values underlying our behaviour, which have become a part of ourselves.

On the motivation continuum, identified and integrated motivations are very close to the intrinsic end, which means the more we develop these types of motivation, the less we need to force ourselves to do things. The closer one moves towards identified and intrinsic motivation, the more authentic and fulfilling one's life becomes.

Tips & Tools
Enhancing your intrinsic motivation
Give yourself a chance to make as many choices as you can, acknowledge how you feel about different situations and whether your point of view differs from that of others. This would enhance your autonomy and, consequently, intrinsic motivation.

Why is autonomy so important for intrinsic motivation? If we are relatively free to choose our actions, then it's easier for us to appreciate the reasons for performing them. However, if we feel forced or compelled to do something, it is more difficult for us to internalize the motivation. That is why offering rewards for activities that should be internally motivated serves to undermine performance and achievement. The other two basic needs of competence and relatedness can also be used as mech-anisms for enhancing intrinsic motivation.

Tips & Tools
Developing integrated motivation in children
Avoid rewarding, forcing or cajoling children to do homework or other desired activities. This may lead to a lack of responsibility. Instead, providing a meaningful rationale for an activity, making it more interesting, empathizing with difficulties, giving plenty of praise, supporting autonomy and being interested and caring are the keys to raising self-motivated kids (Brown & Ryan, 2004).

Life goals

To a great extent, well-being depends on our ability to choose a direc-tion in life, to form intentions and to make sure we are following a certain preferred path (Schmuck & Sheldon, 2001). Life goals – which are also called core goals, personal strivings, personal projects, life tasks and future aspirations – are specific motivational objectives by which we direct our lives. They are not the same as needs because they are formu-lated at the conscious level. They differ from values one may hold. They are also distinct from short-term goals because they direct people's lives for an extended duration. Research has found that knowing what life goals one is pursuing, why one is pursuing them, and how well these goals correspond with one's values can help improve the quality of one's life.

The *self-concordance model* claims that well-being is higher when people select goals that are based on identified, integrated and intrinsic motivation (see previous section) (Sheldon, 1994). Not only are self-concordant goals associated with higher hedonic and eudaimonic well-being, but people are also more likely to sustain efforts to achieve them, as longitudinal research demonstrates. When these goals are achieved, well-being becomes enhanced even further. The reason why self-concordant goals promote well-being is because they satisfy innate psychological needs (see previous chapter).

What goals?

Some researchers think that certain goals are more likely to contribute to well-being than others. For example, the humanist Erich Fromm (1976) made a distinction between a 'having orientation' (obtaining wealth and status) and a 'being orientation' (e.g. self-actualization), and found that people with a being orientation are happier on average (Fromm, 1976) [perhaps, because they don't suffer from status anxiety and don't waste their time trying to keep up with the Jones's (De Botton, 2005)]. Many others also think that focusing on extrinsic goals (financial success, social recognition and appearance) is not quite as good an idea as focusing on intrinsic aspirations (e.g. self-acceptance, affiliation and community feeling) (Kasser & Ryan, 1996). Extrinsic goals are associated with lower self-esteem, more drug use, more television watching, more difficult and less satisfying relationships, and acting in a narcissistic and competitive manner.

However, other research (e.g. the *value-as-a-moderator model*) came to somewhat different conclusions, showing that it is not so much the content of the goals themselves that is important, but the congruence between the values a person holds and their goals (Oishi et al., 1999). This particular model explored Schwartz's ten universal values (power, achievement, hedonism, stimulation, self-direction, universalism, benevolence, tradition, conformity and security). Oishi and colleagues did not find that extrinsic values (such as power) or intrinsic values (e.g. benevolence, self-direction) were associated with lower and higher well-being respectively, only that the value-congruent goals and activities provide a sense of satisfaction.

It turns out that if people value money, have materialistic or other resource-related goals (money, health, athletic ability and attractiveness) and manage to obtain these resources, they feel more satisfied than those who don't value these resources (Diener & Fujita, 1995). (We know, nevertheless, that their satisfaction will not last, and they will become accustomed to these resources very quickly.)

So, while the content of goals (like having and being) may be important *per se*, the congruence or how well one's goals match one's values is of no less importance.

Tips & Tools
Managing goals conflict

Goals can conflict with our values, which is what incongruence is about. However, goals can also be in conflict among themselves (e.g. when achievement of one goal blocks the achievement of another). You can establish a dialogue between conflicting goals and see if they can find a common ground.

If the pursuit of goals is so important for well-being, why do people so often fail to pursue them? There are several reasons for this (Ford & Nichols, 1991). First, people often choose to pursue goals that are less important but urgent and attract more attention (daily chores, events, etc.). Second, we fear that we might not be able to accomplish something for one reason or another and, as a consequence, never even try. Finally, sometimes it's just hard to keep going – we may run out of energy and give up before achieving a desired outcome (a high drop-out rate from distance learning institutions is one such example).

Well-being is enhanced when people choose to pursue goals that are:

- feasible, realistic and attainable
- being progressed towards
- personally meaningful
- highly committed to
- intrinsic
- concerned with community, intimacy and growth
- self-concordant and congruent with people's motives and needs
- valued by one's culture
- not conflicting.

(Lyubomirsky, 2001)

You may have noticed that in this chapter that I did not make a distinction between hedonic (happiness) and eudaimonic (personal growth/transcendence) when talking about the impact of goals on well-being. This is because much of the research on goals used traditional measures of well-being (i.e. hedonic). However, there are many reasons to believe that pursuing certain types of goals and having an internal congruence between our goals and values may have an even higher impact on our eudaimonic well-being.

Note

1 Can you think of any other universal values that are not in this list?

Further reading

Deci, E.L., & Ryan, R.M. (Eds.) (2006). *The handbook of self-determination research.* Rochester, NY: University of Rochester Press.

Chapter Eight
Time in Our Lives

Time is an important issue for most of us, especially in the West. We save it, spend it, waste it, we never have enough of it. The concept of 'time famine' has become a familiar slogan in both academic literature and the popular media (Banks, 1983). Thirty-four per cent of people feel rushed all the time, with 61 per cent never having any excess time and 40 per cent saying that time is more a problem for them than money (Robinson & Godbey, 1997). Time has a vicious habit of slipping through our fingers, leaving us with the feeling that instead of being in charge of our own time, it is driving us. We are not just busy at work; we are busy everywhere – at home, on the golf course, even on holidays.

If you were a scientist trying to figure out how to solve the problem of time scarcity, what would you suggest? On the surface, the answer seems quite simple: if we just worked a little bit less and had a little bit more free time, that would release us from this notorious 'busyness' imprisonment. Yet social scientists studying time-use patterns have discovered a paradox: the last four or five decades have already witnessed this desired increase in free time. Although there are some conflicting opinions on this point, it appears that since 1965 we have, on average, gained between five and seven free hours a week (Robinson & Godbey, 1997; Pentland et al., 1999)! Have you noticed? If you haven't, you are not alone. Although research clearly shows that the time devoted to work has declined, it also shows that people actually believe that it has increased. We have more time, yet we feel that we have less. Interestingly, the vast majority of us have a tendency to greatly overestimate the amount of time we spend working and underestimate how much free time we have. On average, people estimate that they have fewer than twenty hours of free time a week, which is about half of what they actually have (Sullivan & Gershuny, 2001).

There is another interesting paradox regarding time. Nowadays, our leisure time is characterized by two contradictory tendencies – an increase in passive leisure and an intensification of time devoted to active leisure. What is the main consumer of our free time? Television! All the increases in our free time have been devoted to television viewing, even though it doesn't give us much pleasure and is associated with boredom, a low level of concentration, a low level of potency, lack of clarity of thought and lack of flow (Csikszentmihalyi, 1992).

While people squander about a third of all free time (more than fourteen hours a week) in front of their TV screens, they spend significantly less time on the activities they themselves consider most pleasurable, such as socializing and outside activities (Tyrrell, 1995). Moreover, when people do engage in active leisure, they just cram a larger number of activities into a shorter period (this phenomenon is called 'time-deepening'). We are no longer satisfied with one hobby – as a society of maximizers, we are reluctant to choose only one activity. Instead of playing golf for a hobby, we play golf and tennis, go sailing and mountain climbing, bungee jumping and parachuting. We choose activities that can be done quickly, speed them up and combine them, so that they take less time individually. We may achieve more but we pay for it with feelings of fragmentation and time strain (Robinson & Godbey, 1997). I like the following quote from Russell: 'To be able to fill leisure intelligently is the last product of civilization, and at present very few people have reached that level' (Lane, 1995: 39).

It appears that the problem in relation to time crunch lies not in the amount of time available, not in having to manage time successfully to squeeze an extra hour out of the day, but in learning how to balance time in such a way that it contributes to our well-being. But how do we do it? What is a good use of time? How can time be managed so that it contributes to well-being? How can the experience of time pressure be avoided so that time is no longer perceived as an enemy? How can we regain a feeling of control over our time? How can we find a balance between work and leisure and satisfaction in both? In this chapter, I consider two aspects of research on the psychology of time – time perspective and time use, and some techniques related to achieving mastery over time. These issues can greatly contribute to answering the positive psychology central question of 'What is a good life?' (Seligman & Csikszentmihalyi, 2000).

Time perspective

Your time perspective is the kind of glasses you habitually put on when you look at the world around you and at yourself in it. These glasses have three main types of lens: past, present and future. Are you a here-and-now person? Do you sometimes think that you are stuck in the past? Choosing between work and play, do you usually go for work because your future depends on it? Time perspective (TP) relates to whether we focus on our past, present or future when we make decisions and take actions. It is a powerful influence on many aspects of our behaviour, including educational achievement, health, sleep, romantic partner choices and more. Although TP may be affected by situational forces, such as inflation, going on holidays or being stressed, it can become a relatively stable personality characteristic. Thus people tend to have one dominant temporal perspective (Zimbardo & Boyd, 1999).

There are five main subtypes of time perspective: future, past-negative, past-positive, present-hedonistic and present-fatalistic (for the scale that measures TP, see Zimbardo and Boyd, 1999). I will give a little flavour of each of them.

The person who is predominantly *future-oriented* is concerned with working for future goals and rewards, often at the expense of present enjoyment, delaying gratification and avoiding time-wasting temptations. People with future TP are more likely to floss their teeth, eat healthy foods and get medical check-ups on time. They also tend to be more successful than others. The third little pig who built his house from bricks, adequately estimating the dangers from the wolf, was surely a future-oriented pig (Boniwell & Zimbardo, 2003).

The *present-hedonistic* person lives in the moment, is a pleasure seeker, enjoys high-intensity activities, seeks thrills and new sensations and loves adventures. Children are primarily present-hedonistically oriented. Unfortunately, such behaviour can have negative consequences. Present-hedonists are at risk of giving into temptations, leading to virtually all addictions (e.g. alcohol and drug abuse), risky driving, accidents and injuries, and academic and career failure. The *present-fatalistic* TP, on the other hand, is associated with helplessness, hopelessness and a belief that outside forces control one's life (e.g. spiritual or governmental forces).

The past TP is associated with a focus on family, tradition, continuity of self over time and a focus on history. This can be either positive or negative. The *past-positive* person has a warm, pleasurable, often sentimental and nostalgic view of one's past, and values maintaining relationships with family and friends. He or she loves stories about the good old times. The *past-negative* person feels haunted by the past, focusing on personal experiences that were aversive or unpleasant.

Like people, even nations and cultures can have their own time perspective biases. Protestant and individualistic nations tend to be more future-oriented than Catholic and more collectivistic ones. The former are usually better off financially than the latter. People living in southern areas are more present-oriented than those in the north (possibly because they like to spend time enjoying the sunshine).

Five little pigs

Time perspective and the Holy Grail of well-being

Which one of the time perspective types do you think is most conducive for well-being? The present-fatalistic and past-negative orientations cannot be considered for obvious reasons. Many researchers claim that a focus on the future is fundamental to well-being and positive functioning (Kahana & Kahana, 1983; Kakazina, 1999; Wills et al., 2001; Zaleski et al., 2001). Yet the drawbacks of an excessive future orientation include workaholism, neglect of friends and family, not taking time for occasional self-indulgence, and not having time for hobbies (Boniwell & Zimbardo, 2004). Many other scholars think that a time orientation with a focus on the present is a prerequisite for well-being. Among them are Schopenhauer, Maslow and Csikszentmihalyi, with their emphasis on the value of here-and-now experiences. However, this orientation has its downsides as well, including the neglect of long-term consequences and 'the morning after' feeling.

Recent research has found that, contrary to expectations, future TP does not show any association with well-being whatsoever, while the present-hedonistic orientation has very modest associations with life satisfaction, although a better relationship with positive affect (which is hardly surprising considering that the present-hedonistic orientation is aimed at maximizing current feelings of joy and excitement) (Drake et al., 2008; Boniwell et al., 2010).

The time perspective that turns out to be most conducive for well-being is the past-positive orientation (Kakazina, 1999; Boniwell et al., 2010). Past-positive oriented individuals have the highest self-esteem and are satisfied with their past and present life. However, even this very positive perspective has its own drawbacks, which include being excessively conservative or cautious, avoiding change and openness to new experiences and cultures, sustaining the status quo – even when it is not in one's best interest – and trying to apply old solutions to new problems. Is developing the past-positive TP the best one could do?

Tips & Tools
Getting rid of temporal biases
Which time perspective is dominant in your own life? Do you always find it helpful as a response to the situation? What do you think are the disadvantages of your temporal orientation? Try doing something opposite to what you usually do. For example, if you are chronically future-oriented, you may benefit from permitting yourself to take some time off, whereas if you are present-hedonistically oriented, you may benefit from making some long-term plans. If you wish to enhance the past-positive mode, give an old friend a ring, have a game of 'Snakes & Ladders' with children, or browse through a photo album.

Balanced time perspective

Each of the TP types may have some personal value, but if it becomes excessive and excludes or minimizes the others, then it may become dysfunctional. As shown above, there are costs and sacrifices associated with emphasizing any individual TP, whether the focus is on achievement-oriented, 'workaholic' future TP; hedonistic-present or nostalgic-past (which is an infrequent TP in modern society). Here is where the ideal of a *balanced* time perspective comes into play. It is proposed as a more positive alternative to being a slave to any particular temporal bias. 'In an optimally balanced time perspective, the past, present and future components blend and flexibly engage, depending on a situation's demands and our needs and values' (Zimbardo, 2002: 62).

What does it mean to have a balanced TP? Our research shows that people with a balanced time perspective profile tend to score higher than usual on the future and past-positive time perspective scales, have average or slightly below-average scores on the present-hedonistic scale, combined with low past-negative and present-fatalistic scores. What this means is that people with a balanced time perspective are capable of adopting a temporal perspective appropriate to the situation they find themselves in. So when they spend time with their families and friends, they are fully with them, connecting and enjoying each other. When they take a day off work, they can rest rather than feel restless. However, when working and studying they approach a situation from the perspective of the future and work more productively. A capacity to focus, flexibility and 'switchability' are essential components of a balanced TP. Although a balanced TP is hard to achieve, it offers a key to work–life balance and a sense of well-being. Our research shows that people with a balanced TP are happier than the rest of population, in terms of both hedonic and eudaimonic well-being, scoring higher on measures of satisfaction with life, positive affectivity, subjective happiness, optimism, self-efficacy, self-actualization, purpose in life and time competence (Boniwell et al., 2010).

Although at present there are no empirical studies demonstrating this connection, a balanced time perspective sits well with the idea of *time affluence* (vs. *time poverty*) proposed by Tim Kasser. His research shows that people with shorter work hours (i.e. not stuck in the future time perspective behaviours!) are more satisfied with life, engage in more positive environmental behaviours, and have smaller ecological footprints (Kasser & Sheldon, 2009).

Tips & Tools
Time affluence

Given that striving for material affluence is not going to improve our happiness, perhaps we should focus on time affluence instead. Ask a person you live with to say 'time poverty' every time you complain about being rushed, overworked or behind. If it looks like your time poverty is higher than you would like it to be, find one thing you can do to be more in the positive-past or present zone and do it!

Using time wisely

Have you ever been on a time management course? How many time management tricks did you learn? How many of them have you used since? Contrary to popular belief, research shows that time management training has very little effect on our time use and performance (Macan et al., 1990; Macan, 1994, 1996). We tend to revert to our usual ways of organizing time within weeks of attending such training. This is quite amazing, taking into account the financial and other resources invested by companies in these courses. Their failure to produce the desired results may be attributed to focusing on the wrong thing – behaviour rather than psychology of time.

Tips & Tools

Mechanics of time management

Don't get overly enthusiastic about time management tricks, such as diaries, lists, ticks, palm-held electronic organizers, etc. Even if you succeed at sticking to the latest craze, this is not what gives one a sense of satisfaction with time. The 'tyranny of the to-do list' has the capacity to paralyse us over and above the help these lists can offer. Yes, organizing/ prioritizing IS important, but it needs to be flexible, sensitive to your energy and needs, and perceived as a choice rather than an imposition.

Principles of time management

Let us now consider what actually does have an effect on how well we use time, how satisfied we feel with it and how much we are in control of it (Boniwell, 2009).

- Time use, like more or less anything else in life, starts with motivation. How well we use it will depend on how motivated we are to engage in certain activities. This is why *liking what you do and perceiving it as worthwhile* is the first principle of time management. This principle also draws on the sense of congruence between one's life goals and one's life activities and corresponds to intrinsic and incorporated motivation (see Chapter 7). It's important to make sure that you are engaged in activities you either like doing or, as far as the activities you don't like quite as much are concerned, you really know why you are doing them. If you cannot subscribe fully to the values underlying your behaviour, it might be more beneficial for your own well-being to reconsider your choice of activities.

- The principle of *balance* reflects a balance between bound and freely chosen activities, between different areas of one's life. A balanced use of time does not mean equal allocation of time to work and leisure; it does not even necessarily mean investing more time into leisure. A sense of balance is subjective and varies greatly between people. For one person, spending an hour a week on their favourite hobby is sufficient, while for another an hour a day is not enough. There are two other components of this balance principle thar are worth paying attention to. The first is having some time for yourself on a daily basis – time that can be used to stop and reflect. There is a very strong message emanating from research – people who are satisfied with their time make some time for themselves regularly (it can be anything, from doing yoga or going to the gym to meditating or just pottering around the house in peace). The second component concerns the boundary system adopted by an individual. We tend to think that it's vitally important to strictly demarcate the boundaries between work and home, work and leisure, etc., yet it does not matter what boundary system an individual chooses (it can be a strict demarcation or no boundaries at all). What does matter is whether it suits their nature.

- The *responsibility and achievement* principle means adopting a proactive rather than a reactive attitude in relation to time, and preventing oneself from feeling over-stressed (which can be achieved through prioritizing and making choices). It refers also to having a sense of achievement. When people talk about time, they talk about achievement – completion, meeting deadlines and feeling progress. It can be difficult to have a sense of achievement on a daily basis, especially when you are working on a long-term project. To compensate, it is important to complete something every day – it may be something very simple, like tidying up a desk or helping your child to finish homework.

- *Time anxiety and lack of control* is an upside-down principle of time management, reflecting something that needs to be conquered. It is about feeling that time is running out and of not being able to exercise any control over it, feelings that are voiced by most people who are dissatisfied with their time. These can be counteracted by developing an internal locus of control (e.g. through visualization and other techniques).

This list of principles is not necessarily exhaustive, but it is what I can wholeheartedly recommend on the basis of my own research into time management.

Further reading

Boniwell, I., Osin, E., Linley, P.A., & Ivanchenko, G. (2010). A question of balance: Examining relationships between time perspective and measures of well-being in the British and Russian student samples. *Journal of Positive Psychology*, 5, 24–40.

Zimbardo, P. (2008). *The time paradox: The new psychology of time that will change your life*. New York: Simon & Schuster.

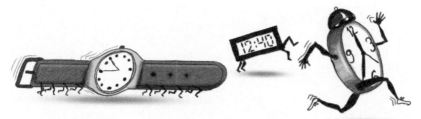

Chapter Nine
Positive Psychology and Life
Complexities and Challenges

Stress, limitations, challenging situations, loss, significant life changes such as ageing, and even death are an inevitable part of being human. Although on the surface these issues sound like nemeses of positive psychology, some argue that instead of ignoring them, positive psychology should study how managing them can contribute to a life well lived.

Dealing with adversity

Coping strategies

When we become stressed, we use different ways to cope with adverse or challenging situations. Researchers organize these coping strategies into three broad groups: problem-focused, emotion-focused and avoidant coping (Carr, 2004). *Problem-focused coping* happens when people identify the problem and take steps to resolve it. These strategies aim to modify the source of stress directly, sorting the problem out. *Emotion-focused coping* is focused not so much on the problem but on the emotions it arouses in us. So, when we turn to someone else for assistance, it is generally for emotional support (e.g. talking things through, crying, empathy), rather than instrumental (e.g. specific advice on what to do in the situation). It often pays to deal with the emotions first, before focusing on the actual problem at hand. When the emotions have been diffused, we can think better and evaluate the situation more accurately, seeing the opportunities in it. These strategies are also more appropriate for uncontrollable stresses, such as bereavement, when it is impossible to 'solve' the problem. *Avoidance coping* happens when people try to deny that the problem exists, and try to block it out of their minds (possibly with the help of alcohol, drugs, sex or even work).

The concrete strategies in these three broad groups can be functional and dysfunctional. For example, accepting responsibility for solving a problem and developing a realistic action plan are among the functional problem-focused strategies, while procrastination and pessimism are among the dysfunctional ones. Similarly, catharsis, emotional discharge or asking friends for support are the constructive emotion-focused ways of coping, while getting involved in destructive relationships, aggression or wishful thinking are much less so. Avoidance-focused strategies also can be useful in the short term. It may be a good idea to go to the movies or play pool with friends to distract you from a pressing problem for an evening. However, being permanently distracted and mentally disengaged from it is dysfunctional, partly because unattended problems do not sort themselves out but tend to become worse with time.

Adaptive defence mechanisms

If coping strategies are something that we consciously engage in, psycho-analysts claim that we also have certain unconscious processes that assist us in recovering from life's stresses. These unconscious processes, called *adaptive defence mechanisms*, are positive and very useful. They include anticipation, affiliation, humour, self-assertion, self-observation, subli-mation and suppression. Just to give some examples, anticipation prepares us emotionally for potentially unfavourable outcomes of chal-lenging situations. Affiliation leads us to pick up the phone and chat to a friend about a hard day at work, without deliberately using it as a coping strategy. Reframing negative situations into humorous ones is a common and very effective mechanism. Sublimation allows us to transform negative reactions (e.g. aggression) or strong natural urges (e.g. sexual desire) into constructive activities. All of these defences tend to develop and become more effective as our lives progress. The more we use them, the better our adaptation and resilience will become (Vaillant, 2000).

While both functional coping strategies and adaptive defence mechanisms are very helpful, the dividing line between them is rather vague, and there are some overlaps when it comes to the particulars. For example, if we become aware of our defence mechanisms, don't they automatically relocate into the deliberate strategies camp?

Post-traumatic growth

We encounter stresses on a daily basis, some of them more severe than others. However, at times we are faced with traumatic events that have the potential to change the course of our lives for ever. It may be the tsunami that took or ruined the lives of thousands on Boxing Day 2004; it may be genocide, like that in Rwanda; rape, sexual abuse, learning that one is HIV-positive or has terminal cancer, losing a loved one, perhaps a child, giving birth to a heavily disabled baby, losing one's home in a fire, or losing a limb.

These (and, unfortunately, many other devastating events) can shatter our very picture of the world. Certain beliefs (e.g. people are good or the world is just) may no longer ring true, many goals may no longer be important. Yet, even when this happens, some individuals emerge from the experience having *gained* something from it. This phenomenon is called *post-traumatic growth*. Many people feel that they are much stronger following the adversity, and have more confidence in themselves and their capacities. Others report improved and stronger relationships (trauma often acts like a litmus paper, revealing the value of your relationships), or having greater compassion for others in similar situations. Sometimes people learn to appreciate anew what they have, even the small things in life that we so often take for granted. Moreover, some individuals discover meaning or spirituality in the aftermath of the event, leading to the development of a more coherent and satisfying worldview and life philosophy (Tedeschi & Calhoun, 2004).

Many religious scholars, philosophers and writers have emphasized the positive that can be found in suffering. Among them are theologians from the Christian, Buddhist, Hindu and Islamic traditions and thinkers like Nietzsche, Dante, Dostoyevsky and Solzhenitsyn (Joseph & Linley, 2005). The Austrian psychiatrist Viktor Frankl wrote a book entitled *Man's Search for Meaning* (1963) about his experiences in a Nazi concentration camp. The book is a tribute to finding humanity and meaningfulness even in the midst of despair, when all the attributes of existence (identity, possessions, loved ones, even the right to live) have been taken away.

So how do we move from such traumatic experiences to growing as people? The process usually starts with attempting to make sense of what happened. This takes place almost automatically as people try to work out which steps and coincidences have led to the event. Then comes an attempt to remake sense of life as a whole, or *cognitive restructuring*. The internal world has to be rebuilt anew, often with major alterations in one's view, even of oneself. This process is more deliberate. If it is absent, and the assimilation of the traumatic experience into one's life picture does not happen, the person may not be able to come to terms with the event and may also be vulnerable to future negative occurrences.

Frankl believed that the *attitude* an individual adopts towards adversity is absolutely crucial for successful adjustment (Nolen-Hoeksema & Davis, 2002): 'Everything can be taken from a man but . . . the last of the human freedoms – to choose one's attitude in any given set of circumstances, to choose one's own way' (Frankl, 1963: 104). If a traumatic situation is interpreted as a challenge, the person is more likely to experience post-traumatic growth.

Finally, another crucial factor is *interpersonal support*. Assisted by sympathetic interpersonal connections, which encourage and allow disclosure and growth, a person has a much better chance to adjust successfully (Linley & Joseph, 2004a).

Interestingly, post-traumatic growth is associated with not only better psychological but also physical health. For example, HIV-positive men who actively engage in meaning-making after the loss of their partners have much better immunological indicators of disease progression two to three years after the event than those who do not (Baumeister & Vohs, 2002).

It's important to note that growth and distress often co-exist. In fact, it may be the balance between recognition of gains and losses that leads to the best adjustment (Tennen & Affleck, 2002). This, of course, is not to say that trauma is necessary for growth. Trauma is not good and cannot be good *per se*, but it can bring about meaningful personal changes (Tennen & Affleck, 2002). A person may become even wiser as a result of post-traumatic growth, which is our next subject.

Wisdom

Wisdom is something that can assist us in dealing with challenging and complex situations (Baltes, 1987). Wisdom can be facilitative of post-traumatic growth and can also grow from it (Linley & Joseph, 2004a), although, of course, traumatic events are not necessary to become wise.

Currently, there are two dominant theories of wisdom within positive psychology: Berlin's wisdom paradigm and Sternberg's balance theory of wisdom.

Berlin's wisdom paradigm

Berlin's paradigm defines wisdom as knowledge about fundamental life pragmatics, including concern with the conduct, purpose and meaning of life (Baltes & Freund, 2003).

Five criteria are seen to be essential for wisdom: (1) rich factual knowledge about pragmatics (or facts) of life – having a truly superior

information base; (2) rich knowledge of how to deal with these pragmatics – 'know how' to make decisions, resolve conflicts, etc.; (3) knowledge about many themes and contexts of life, including self, family,
school, workplace, and understanding how they are interrelated, how
they change and affect each other; (4) recognition and tolerance
of differences in beliefs and values (this does not imply relativism of
values); (5) recognition and management of uncertainty and tolerance of
ambiguity (accepting that knowledge has limits and we can never predict
with total accuracy what will happen in the future). Someone with
deep knowledge about life can be considered wise if all these five criteria
are met.

Importantly, wisdom does not depend on superior cognitive or
technical knowledge. Wisdom is a combination of intellectual aspects
and a deep understanding of affect and motivation. Experience (and
training) in dealing with complex life problems enhances the development of wisdom (Kunzmann, 2004).

The researchers in Berlin's wisdom group found that, contrary to
popular beliefs, wisdom can characterize people of any age (Baltes et al.,
1995). While wisdom rapidly increases during adolescence and young
adulthood, it may not rise any further during the adult years.

Sternberg's balance theory of wisdom

According to this theory, wisdom is a combination of practical intelligence and tacit knowledge, applied to solving problems for the common
good (Reznitskaya & Sternberg, 2004). This tacit element, as emphasized by Aristotle, Sternberg interprets as flexibility and an ability to
appreciate nuances that cannot be learnt from any formalized set of
rules. This model places a strong accent on balance.

For example, wisdom involves balancing among multiple interests,
including the intrapersonal (or own), interpersonal (of other people
around you) and extrapersonal (things that would be good for everyone,
wider organizations, community, country, environment). Wisdom also

involves balance between different ways in which we can respond to the situation and our environment. For instance, faced with the same situation, we can *adapt* to it, *shape* it so it adapts to us, or *select* a new environment that is more conducive to our needs and actions.

Wisdom is usually applied to deal with complex problems involving multiple competing interests and multiple response strategies. The outcome of wisdom is a judgement or advice on how these problems can be solved in such a way that the common good is satisfied (Carr, 2004).

Tips & Tools

Awakening wisdom

Create an image that represents wisdom for you and engage in a dialogue with it. It can be a sage, philosopher, an old friend, relative or teacher (Popovic, 2005).

Both of the above models seem to have their merits. An emphasis on balance is undoubtedly important; however, a notion of 'common good' carries an inherent value judgement. The Berlin paradigm seems comprehensive, but lacks the essential tacit component of wisdom and appears rather complicated. Neither of the models mentions what may be one of the most important components of wisdom: a capacity to foresee the long-term consequences of one's actions.

Positive ageing

The ageing process is a major challenge that most of us will encounter sooner or later. The good news is – we are living longer nowadays. The bad news – ageing does not seem to be held in high respect in the media and popular culture. When asked to describe the first image that comes to mind when they think of an older person, most people say 'wise', 'slow', 'ill', 'infirm' or 'frail' (Lupien & Wan, 2004). In fact, we know from the previous section that wisdom is not connected with age (our common perception is wrong here), so how correct are our other stereotypes (which, incidentally, are all negative)? We eagerly count 'the wrinkles of age'. Ageing is associated with decline in physical and sensory functioning, impaired hearing, vision, capacity to taste and savour. Deterioration of cognitive abilities and a struggle to remember names are also emphasized. Reduction in social interactions and eventual loneliness seem also to be part of this inevitable process. Yet, do they have to be?

Research data shows that most adults over 65 are very healthy. A large survey carried out in the mid-1990s demonstrated that 73 per cent of people between 78 and 84 years reported no disabling conditions, and 40 per cent of those over 85 reported being in a similar state of health (Williamson, 2002). Contrary to the existing stereotypes, many physical problems can be eliminated with good diet and exercise. It is never too late to start living healthily – our bodies are unbelievably forgiving. Within five years, for example, all the negative effects of even very heavy smoking can be reversed. Proper maintenance can do miracles!

Even declining cognitive performance (including memory) can be improved with quite modest training. In fact, an older adult's brain continues to produce new neurons, and does not lose as many old ones as was once thought (Lupien & Wan, 2004). It can even learn new things fairly well. The 'use it or lose it' expression is very relevant here, as well as being applicable to sexual functioning. But what is fundamentally important for maintaining effective cognitive functioning is the belief that one can learn and remember.

The American psychiatrist George Vaillant followed two groups of men for over thirty years (from the time before they were 50 to their 70s and 80s), studying their ageing processes. He discovered six factors that (contrary to expectations) did not predict healthy ageing: ancestral longevity (how long one's parents lived), cholesterol level, parental social class, warm childhood environment, stable childhood tempera-ment (rated by parents) and stress. What does predict good healthy ageing, however, are the following seven factors: not being a heavy smoker or stopping smoking young (by about the age of 45), mature adaptive defences (discussed earlier in the chapter), absence of alcohol abuse (moderate drinking is perfectly fine), healthy weight, stable marriage, exercise and years of education (the more, the better).

It sounds like – with a bit of work and in the absence of unpredictable events (such as being struck by lightning) – successful ageing is a matter of some effort and not taking it too seriously. Moreover, not only can many of the negatives associated with ageing be avoided, older age can bring some positives and potential strengths (Carstensen & Charles, 2003).

For example, older people have a lower likelihood of clinical depression than younger individuals. They also experience fewer negative emotions than younger people, but a similar number of positive emotions. They exhibit a greater emotional complexity (e.g. joy and sadness can be inter-mixed) and more contentment. They form deeper and closer bonds with people and derive more satisfaction from relationships. While there is a decrease in the number of social interactions, this is because there is less contact with unimportant acquaintances, not because less time is spent in fulfilling contacts. Because time becomes more meaningful, older people select contacts more carefully and strategically. These deep social engagements are protective against cognitive impairment, such as dementia. Older people tend to have an intact memory for emotionally important material. They are better in interpersonal interactions, and better able to see interpersonal problems from multiple perspectives. For example, when discussing conflicts, older couples show fewer negative emotions and more affection towards their partners than younger ones (Carstensen et al., 1995). What seems to make a real difference is the extent of older people's engagement with life. Managing to maintain normal, personally meaningful activities (whether intellectual, physical or social) is seen as another key to successful ageing. For example, researchers have observed a much more successful ageing process and longevity in Kibbutz communities. Because retirement does not equate to stopping work, responsibilities are preserved, jobs tend to become adjusted to changing abilities, and there is widespread social support (Lupien & Wan, 2004).

Feeling in control, being able to make choices and having a positive attitude are also of paramount importance (Person et al., 1988). People who perceive themselves to be younger than others of the same age have a higher level of internal control. Positive attitudes are associated with good memory, longevity, good health, well-being and a will to live.

Contrary to popular expectations, ageing does not need to become an unpleasant experience. Positive ageing can 'add more life to years, not just years to life' (Vaillant, 2004: 561). Rather than seeing ageing as a negative process, a more appropriate conclusion, perhaps, is that all stages in life have their strengths and gains, together with weaknesses and losses. It's just how we look at it. We usually don't focus on the negatives of childhood, such as dependency, lack of freedom, lack of knowledge and intellectual capacities, so why would we focus on the negatives of ageing? The changes brought by the ageing process are best approached as challenges, which can be successfully tackled with appropriate attitudes and maintenance, and transformed into something we can benefit from.

Further reading

Vaillant, G.E. (2002). *Aging well*. Boston, MA: Little, Brown.

Chapter Ten
The Freedom of Choice and How to Survive it

In 1970, Alvin Toffler wrote a book entitled *Future Shock*, which became a seminal sociological masterpiece on what future is to come and how we can possibly learn to deal with it. The term 'future shock' refers to what happens when people are no longer able to cope with the profound and rapid changes and enormous amounts of information the super-industrial revolution brings with it. Written nearly forty years ago, the book is still current today, contrary to the logic that nothing ages faster than futuristic books. Although not all of Toffler's forecasts came true, many did: students today are the creators of their own mix-and-match degrees, marriages at eighteen 'until the death parts us' are long-gone fairytales of the past, and homosexual marriages with children are just another form of a family unit accepted in civilized societies.

One of the main threads running through the book is that of overchoice and freedom that might, in a somewhat counter-intuitive way, take our very freedom away. In the midst of anxiety about underchoice and increasing standardization of the early 1970s, Toffler warns of an unparalleled surfeit of choice, resulting from increases in affluence and technological sophistication. The early indicators for such a prediction were already there. Between 1950 and 1963, the number of soaps and detergents sold by American supermarkets rose from 65 to 200. In the 1970s, a person buying a car would have needed to spend several days learning about various brands, models and options to make a decision. The industry was already in danger of producing more diversity than a buyer would need or want.

Toffler painted a gloomy picture of a society in which 'overchoice' becomes the norm. Decisions become harder and require much more work. We need time to collect and research all the relevant information about even the most trivial matters, such as choosing a washing machine (or a mobile phone, nowadays). Therefore, an increase in the number of choices leads to an increase in the amount of information that needs to be processed. Practice confirms the experimental findings, in which the more choices one has, the slower one reacts. More than that, the accelerating tempo of life requires that we process information at a far more rapid pace than ever before. With the overload in the amount and speed of information, we experience cognitive overstimulation. We become paralysed, struggling to choose and decide. Decisions come at a high psychological cost, which can lead to depression, personality disorder, neurosis and psychological distress. In the end, the advantages of diversity and individualization become cancelled out by the complexity of the consumer's decision-making process. Toffler (1970: 257–258) writes:

> Whether man is prepared to cope with the increased choice of material and cultural wares available to him is, however, a totally different question. For there comes a time when choice, rather than freeing the individual, becomes so complex, difficult and costly, that it turns into its opposite. There comes a time, in short, when choice turns into overchoice and freedom into un-freedom.

In 2000, a professor of psychology in Swarthmore College in the USA, Barry Schwartz, published an article entitled 'Self-determination: The tyranny of freedom'.[1] In it, he speaks of the psychological problems of freedom and autonomy, arguing that more choice is not necessarily good, and, in fact, often makes our lives worse, rather than better. Sounds familiar? Unfortunately, in the positive psychology tradition, he has omitted the good work and genius of Alvin Toffler. Leaving aside the lack of such an acknowledgement, however, Schwartz's (2000) argument echoes and extends that of Toffler.

Overchoice is no longer a fear but a reality (Schwartz & Ward, 2000). In 2004, your local supermarket was likely to be storing approximately

360 types of shampoo, conditioner, gel and mousse. We have to, willingly or unwillingly, exercise choice when we go shopping, take up a pension plan, choose a telephone provider, decide how to work (part-time, full-time, flexible hours, from home, while travelling, etc.), decide what type of relationship to enter, and so on. Even personal identity is a choice. For example, I can choose to identify myself as: Latvian, Russian, British, European, a citizen of the world, not to mention as a young woman, a mother or a scholar. Who am I? Any or all of the above!

In the Western world, freedom, autonomy and choice are considered to be the conditions of psychological health (see the self-determination model in Chapter 6). Yet what we see alongside is a phenomenal growth of depression and suicide, especially among the young (Popovic, 2002). Freedom doesn't come cheap. We have to pay for it by exercising responsibility. Choices are costly too, with the price for them measured in decisions.

The widespread availability of choice and freedom leads, according to Schwartz, to three major problems:

- *Information problems* – how can we access all information about all alternatives so as to make an informed choice?
- *Error problems* – with more complex options, we are more likely to make errors of judgement.
- *Psychological problems* – excess choice causes one to worry. It does not appear to lead to greater psychological well-being; in fact, quite the opposite – increased choice is accompanied by decreased well-being.

Several experiments have shown that, instead of being liberating, choice can be demotivating. In one such experiment, participants were invited into a gourmet supermarket to taste a variety of jams. One group of people tasted six different types of jam, another twenty-four, all of which were available for purchase. Thirty per cent of people from the first group actually bought a jar, compared with just 3 per cent from the second group (Jyengar & Lepper, 2000). In another study, two sets of students tasted and rated six or thirty different types of chocolates, respectively. Those tasting six were more satisfied with their tasting than those tasting thirty. These are completely counter-intuitive findings. Surely the more choice there is, the more chance you have to find something you really like? Surely you are free to ignore the other options?

Unfortunately, thinking that you can ignore other options may be logically true, but it is not true psychologically. We get lost in the array of choices open to us. Schwartz rightly notes: 'the fact that *some* choice is good doesn't necessarily mean that *more* choice is better' (Schwartz & Ward, 2004: 87).

In fact, an overload of choice may even lead to a rapid reduction in choices made. Those who watched the UK Channel 4 TV series about the celebrity chef Jamie Oliver trying to introduce healthy (and tasty!) eating in schools, would have noticed how incredibly limited the diets of many children were. Many of them had never tried strawberries, and could not recognize asparagus. And these children lived in the British world of nearly unlimited choice! How can this be the case? With such availability of choice, there is very little chance to make an informed decision, so many parents rely on advertisements to direct their purchasing, becoming slaves to commercials. Neither Toffler nor Schwartz seems to have noticed that the problems of excess choice and standardization can go hand in hand. Standardization (which is more viable economically for manufacturers) is one possible response to the problem of overchoice. Standardization as a response of buyers leads to further standardization of products, accompanied by diversification within these products. This is why one can find at least 15–20 types of orange juice in UK supermarkets, but not a single type of pear or cherry juice.

Personality response to the problem of overchoice

All of us decision-makers can be divided into two general groups: satisficers and maximizers. *Satisficers* are people who just need to get what is 'good enough' for their requirements. They consider options until they find what meets their minimum criteria, and then select that option. *Maximizers* are those who need to get absolutely the best deal and so look at all possible options. Choice overload is a particular problem for maximizers, who want to go to the best college, get the best job, have the best car and wear the best clothes. As more options become available, they need to work harder to exhaust all the possibilities.

Maximization trap

Maximization doesn't come cheap – if you want the best, you should expect to pay the most. The following are the costs of maximization (Schwartz & Ward, 2004):

- *Regret*, actual and anticipated, about not getting the 'best deal'. What if the alternatives are actually better? What if I will regret buying this car?
- *Opportunity costs*. These are the costs of options that are lost by pursuing maximization. Every choice we make has its own opportunity cost.
- *Escalation of expectations*. With more choice, maximizers tend to expect even more.
- *Self-blame*. There is no excuse for a fiasco in a world where everything is possible. Maximizers combine intensely high expectations with personal responsibility for failure.
- *Time*. The time spent choosing kitchen units is the time that could have been spent with children or close friends.

In all honesty, maximizers usually end up doing better in life, but satisficers feel better. The starting salary of maximizers is on average US$7000 per year higher. Yet, they are less satisfied than satisficers with the job they have got. This is how more can end up being less, or at least so costly that it's simply not worth it.

TABLE 10.1 MAXIMIZATION

MAXIMIZATION IS POSITIVELY ASSOCIATED WITH:	MAXIMIZATION IS NEGATIVELY ASSOCIATED WITH:
Regret, perfectionism, depression, upward social comparison (with 'better' people), neuroticism	Happiness, optimism, satisfaction with life, self-esteem

What can be done?

This is where we turn positive and see how normal people can be saved from the tyranny of choice. In *Future Shock*, Toffler (1970) suggests several ways of coping:

- We can temporarily 'freeze-up' decision-making to recover from an overload of sensory and cognitive stimulation.
- We can maintain long-term relationships with the objects from our physical environment. 'Thus we can refuse to purchase throw-away products. We can hang on to the old jacket for another season; we can stoutly refuse to follow the latest fashion trend; we can resist when the salesman tells us it's time to trade in our auto-mobile' (p. 341).
- We can create 'stability zones' to balance the chaos and rapid changes in other parts of our lives. Long-term relationships, employment or daily habits can become such non-changing and stable elements.

Schwartz also offers some useful pointers (Schwartz & Ward, 2004):

- We can learn to satisfice more, accept 'good enough' (e.g. not worry about getting the best trainers, teachers, extra activities for kids but worry about being there for them).

- We can lower our expectations. The reality of any experience can suffer from comparisons. Unfulfilled but unreasonably high expectations are the yellow brick road to depression.
- We can avoid social comparisons and set our own standards.
- We can regret less and be grateful for what is good in life.
- We can practise meta-choice and learn when choosing is worth it. This way we will only be a maximizer when it comes to something that really matters.
- We should try to stick to our choices and not change our minds. This is another way to reduce anxiety.
- We can learn to love constraints. Perhaps some constraints (imposed by relationships, having kids and having a regular job) are a blessing, because they reduce our sets of possible choices. If we create and follow a rule for something, we don't need to make decisions.

And, finally, let's remember that choice only increases freedom up to a certain point, beyond which it actually restricts our freedom.

Note

1 He has since written a number of other articles on this subject as well as a book entitled *The Paradox of Choice: Why More is Less* (Schwartz, 2004).

Further reading

Schwartz, B. (2004). *The paradox of choice: Why more is less.* New York: Ecco Press.

Chapter Eleven
The Positive Psychology of Strengths

The value of strengths

If I asked you to name your strengths, what would you answer? Most people are reluctant to talk about their strengths and many do not even know what they are. This is not just a British phenomenon, a similar picture can be observed in most European and Asian countries. But are strengths at all important? Surely, rather than boasting about what you are good at, it would be better to address your shortcomings.

The initiators of the strengths movement argue from a very different position (Hodges & Clifton, 2004). They believe that two widespread assumptions about human nature are wrong. The first is that everyone can learn to be competent in almost anything. The second is that the greatest potential for growth is in the area of a person's greatest weakness.[1]

Moreover, it is often assumed that top achievers set high goals and low achievers set low goals. However, research indicates that top achievers know their capabilities and set their goals slightly above their current level of performance, whereas low achievers are unaware of their abilities and often set unrealistically high goals. Essentially, top achievers build their personal lives and careers on their talents and strengths. They learn to recognize their talents and develop them further. They find the roles that suit them best and they invent ways to apply their talents and strengths in their lives. As far as weaknesses are concerned, they manage rather than develop them (Clifton & Anderson, 2001–02).

Cross-cultural research on the value of strengths suggests that knowing and following your strengths:

- encourages insight and perspective in your life
- makes one less sensitive to stress
- generates optimism and resilience
- provides a sense of direction
- helps to develop confidence and self-esteem
- generates a sense of vitality and energy
- engenders a sense of happiness and fulfilment
- helps achieve one's goals
- enables one to be more engaged at work and perform better (Clifton & Anderson, 2001–02).

Moreover, the development of certain strengths helps build resilience and buffers against some types of dysfunction and mental disorders. For example, optimism buffers against depression; flow in sports against substance abuse; work ethics and social skills against schizophrenia. Courage, future-mindedness, faith, hope, honesty and perseverance are among other buffering strengths.

Some researchers even think that the strengths approach underlies most successful psychological therapies. Good therapists, regardless of their theoretical orientation, use similar strategies in their work with clients, including the *instilling of hope* and *building of buffering strengths*, rather than just delivering damage-healing techniques (Seligman & Peterson, 2003).

Strengths are at the very core of the agenda of positive psychology, because they relate to understanding the plus side of the life equation – the presence of psychological health, rather than the mere absence of psychological illness.

There are three major approaches to the concept of strengths and their measurement: the VIA Classification of Strengths and Virtues, Gallup's StrengthsFinder and CAPP's Realise2.

voluntary domain. The VIA also claims that strengths are morally valued across cultures, whereas talents are non-moral. Moreover, talents are not as buildable as strengths (you are unlikely to improve your pitch or speed as much as you can your bravery, optimism, etc.) (Seligman, 2002). While someone can waste or do nothing with their talent, it would be rather unusual to hear that someone did nothing with their gratitude, for example.

Table 11.1 summarizes strengths and virtues, according to the VIA (Peterson & Seligman, 2004). Allocation of strengths into these categories appears, however, to be quite arbitrary. Forgiveness, which is currently in temperance, may be better placed in justice. Gratitude, humour and appreciation of beauty appear to be rather loosely linked to transcendence. Indeed, which strength falls into which virtue does not seem to be set in stone. Zest, for example, moved between 2001 (when

TABLE 11.1 STRENGTHS AND VIRTUES ACCORDING TO THE VIA

WISDOM AND KNOWLEDGE

- *Curiosity and interest in the world* (being interested in a variety of subjects and experiences)

- *Love of learning* (increasing knowledge for its own sake)

- *Perspective, wisdom* (seeing the big picture, being considered wise)

- *Creativity, ingenuity, originality* (finding new ways to do things, having common sense)

- *Open-mindedness, critical thinking* (being a rational thinker, being able to make good judgements)

(Continued)

TABLE 11.1 *Continued*

COURAGE

- *Valour, bravery* (making a stand, overcoming fear)

- *Persistence, perseverance, industry* (finishing what was started, not getting sidetracked)

- *Integrity, authenticity, honesty* (keeping promises, being genuine and open)

- *Zest, enthusiasm, vitality* (living life to the full, having energy)

LOVE AND HUMANITY

- *Capacity to love and be loved* (valuing and having intimate loving relationships)

- *Kindness, generosity* (helping others, showing empathy, caring)

- *Social intelligence, personal intelligence, emotional intelligence* (sensing what other people feel, awareness of one's own feelings, being at ease with others)

JUSTICE

- *Citizenship, teamwork, loyalty* (working well in a group)

- *Leadership* (organizing and motivating other people)

- *Fairness, equity* (treating people equally, not discriminating on the basis of your own biases)

TEMPERANCE

- *Self-control, self-regulation* (controlling emotions, discipline)

- *Prudence, caution* (avoiding danger, making careful choices)

- *Humility, modesty* (awareness of one's place in a larger universe)

- *Forgiveness, mercy* (forgive and forget attitudes)

TRANSCENDENCE

- *Appreciation of beauty and excellence* (creating it and/or being inspired, elevated by it)

- *Spirituality, sense of purpose, faith, religiousness* (having a calling in life, developing coherent beliefs about the higher meaning)

- *Hope, optimism, future-mindedness* (seeing a glass as half-full, planning for the future)

- *Gratitude* (thanking people, counting blessings)

- *Humour, playfulness* (bringing smiles and laughter, working playfully)

Adapted with permission from Peterson & Seligman (2004) *Character Strengths and Virtues: A Handbook and Classification.*

the classification was developed) and 2004 from transcendence to courage.

One of the major goals of positive psychology is seen to be helping people to identify their *signature* strengths. Signature strengths are those that represent 'the real you', bringing a feeling of excitement when you discover and use them. A person excels in their signature strengths quickly, has a sense of yearning to put them into practice and feels invigorated and intrinsically motivated when using them (Peterson & Seligman, 2004). Once the signature strengths are discovered, they can be applied to areas such as work, relationships, play and parenting (Seligman, 2002).

Gallup's StrengthsFinder

If only the world was simple, and there was just one strengths classification to make sense out of. Unfortunately, simplicity is not a characteristic of our choiceful existence. Just in case twenty-four strengths were not enough, I will now introduce you to thirty-four, identified by the scientists (stroke businessmen) from the Gallup Corporation, Donald Clifton and Edward 'Chip' Anderson (Clifton & Anderson, 2001–02). They endeavoured to understand what makes people excel in what they do through interviewing thousands of top performers across the globe. This led them to come up with thirty-four most prevalent talents/strengths displayed in the work setting. However, their conception of what strengths are is rather different from the picture advocated by the VIA.

According to the StrengthsFinder, the basis of a strength is a *talent*. Talent is a naturally recurring pattern of thought, feeling or behaviour that can be applied to multiple areas. It's a capacity to do something. Talents can be organized into *themes* (groups of similar talents). A *strength* is the ability to provide a consistent, high-level performance in a given activity. If talents are like 'diamonds in the rough', strengths are like diamonds that have been carefully cut and polished. Thus strengths are produced when talents are refined with *knowledge* and *skills*. Strengths that are fully developed and applied appropriately result in achievement and excellence. Certain principles underlie the development and application of strengths:

- understanding of and believing in one's talents
- valuing one's talents and assuming personal responsibility for them
- understanding of one's motivation, knowing why one is doing something; clarification of life goals or objectives
- establishment of caring, facilitative relationships
- reliving previous successes
- practising one's talents and strengths
- teaching others about talents and strengths (this helps one to understand them much better).

Having realized one's talents/strengths, it's important to consider what career is the best match for them. Even the same activity (e.g. studying something) can be approached differently, depending on one's strengths. If your strength is harmony, you might need to start from what you agree with, and then expand from there. If you are analytical, you may start from picking up small nuances of an argument, questioning opinions, refusing to blindly accept what is written, before progressing towards forming a balanced conclusion.

TABLE 11.2 STRENGTHS ACCORDING TO THE GALLUP RESEARCHERS

• *Achievement* (pursuit of goals, productivity, satisfaction from accomplishments)	• *Focus* (determining priorities, finding direction, efficiency)

(Continued)

TABLE 11.2 *Continued*

- *Activation* (energy to get things going and done)

- *Adaptability* (modification of the self depending on the demands of environment; adjustment, flexibility)

- *Being analytical* (understanding of causes and effects; critical thinking)

- *Arrangement* (organization, coordination, identifying the right combination of people and resources)

- *Belief* (having deeply held values, ideas, finding meaning in life)

- *Command* (ability to deal with conflicts and crisis, capacity to be in charge)

- *Communication* (explanation, clarification, good when talking)

- *Competition* (hard work to excel, achievement, desire to win, comparison with others)

- *Future orientation* (focus on the future, seeing possibilities, energizing others)

- *Harmony* (ability to find things in common, avoiding conflicts)

- *Ideation* (creativity, originality, new ideas and concepts)

- *Including* (helping others to be unified and effective)

- *Individualization* (seeing others as individuals and recognizing their talents, focus on the differences)

- *Input* (active knowledge acquisition, curiosity)

- *Intellection* (multiple directions of thinking, intellectual discussions, solutions)

- *Learning* (enjoys learning process, focus on improvement)

- *Maximization* (enhancement of personal and group excellence)

- *Connectedness* (connecting ideas or occurrences into a meaningful whole)

- *Consistency* (equality, fairness, guardianship of 'right and wrong')

- *Context* (seeing historical patterns, perspective)

- *Deliberation* (good decision-making, carefulness, consideration of all options)

- *Development* (seeing potential in others and assisting them in their development)

- *Discipline* (organization, good time-keeping, order and structure)

- *Empathy* (understanding of others, forming supportive relationships)

- *Positivity* (enthusiasm, optimism, excitement, stimulation of others)

- *Relationships* (forming close interpersonal relationships)

- *Responsibility* (person who can be counted on, many obligations and commitments)

- *Restoration* (recognition of problems and ability to fix them)

- *Self-assurance* (self-confidence, independence in thinking)

- *Significance* (high motivation for recognition, hard working)

- *Strategy* (seeing pros and cons and the whole picture, generating appropriate plan of actions)

- *Woo* (quickly connecting with people, forming groups/relationships)

Source: Clifton & Anderson (2001–02).

Tips & Tools
Discovering and applying your strengths
Looking at Table 11.1, which do you think your signature strengths are? You can find out just by giving yourself a score from 1 to 10 for each of the twenty-four strengths. You are not rating how you would like to be, but how you think you are. Pick the strengths with the highest scores (either the top 5 or 6 strengths, or the ones above 8) and ask three more questions for each of them: 'Is this the real me? Do I enjoy using it? Do I find it energizing and exciting?' Once you have claimed ownership of your signature strengths, consider how you can apply them in all the important areas of your life. You can do the same exercise with the Gallup classification in Table 11.2 and compare the results.

CAPP's Realise2

In recent years, a new approach to defining, classifying, measuring and using strengths came to prominence. Developed and marketed by the Centre for Applied Positive Psychology (CAPP), it is quickly becoming the first 'go to' inventory in the UK.

Realise2 went far beyond the other two classifications by offering us the choice of sixty strengths, ranging from Action through to Work Ethic. Given the size of the list, however, it is not presented here, but can be found in the book recommended for this chapter (Linley et al., 2010).

Realise2 has not only maximized the number of strengths, it has enhanced our understanding of these attributes by distinguishing between realized and unrealized strengths, learned behaviours and weaknesses on the basis of whether these energize us, are associated with enhanced performance and are used frequently:

- *Realized strengths* are the things that you already are aware of and use, that energize you, enable you to perform at your best and that you utilize often. You should *marshal* these strengths, by using them appropriately according to the situation and context.

- *Unrealized strengths* are behaviours that you may not be able to use on a daily basis due to your environment and work situation. However, when you do get a chance to use them, you derive energy and satisfaction from exhibiting these attributes. These strengths need to be *maximized*, and opportunities found to develop and use them more.
- *Learned behaviours* encompass the behaviours that you have, over time, learned to perform well; however, you do not derive pleasure or energy from completing them. Instead, you find them de-energizing or perhaps even draining. These behaviours should therefore be *moderated*, used only when you really need to.
- *Weaknesses* encompass all the things that you simply perform poorly at and that drain you of energy. These attributes can create issues and need to be managed or *minimized* so that they do not hinder your being successful in life. This can be done by using one's strengths to compensate, reshaping a work role, finding a complementary partner or even a team, and, when all other methods fail, learning how to develop the weakness so that it is 'good enough' to get by.

Playing to your strengths?

Despite dramatic conceptual differences and rather diverse classifications, the strengths theorists share many assumptions with regard to the usefulness of this concept. They all advocate the introduction of the strengths-based framework in the work setting, measurement of strengths and strengths-based recruitment, and claim that when strengths are played to, individuals can achieve optimal functioning and find performance easier (Linley & Harrington, 2006). It's quite hard to spot any controversies in such a positive agenda. However, there are several points of concern.

First, it is not clear how comprehensive these strengths classifications are. For example, moderation, self-awareness, patience or spontaneity cannot be found in either of the above lists. Perhaps they didn't fit the criteria. But how were these criteria selected and why should we assume that they are valid? By reducing the strengths lists to a manageable number, aren't we simplifying life somewhat, disadvantaging people who have strengths that are not on the list?

Positive psychology advocates questionnaires as the best method to identify one's strengths, but this may not be the case. Years ago, when I first completed the VIA, I was not surprised when 'optimism' was among my top five strengths. It was only after three close people, independently of each other, pointed out to me that I was one of the most pessimistic individuals they had ever met, that I began doubting my 'signature strength'. Joyful and rather future-minded on the surface, but quite pessimistic on the inside, I indeed believed that I was an optimist, and the questionnaire simply reflected my own bias.

While I have little doubt that focusing on what you are already good at enhances achievement, I wonder how it affects the development of a balanced personality. The strengths framework fits beautifully into the American ideology with its underlying belief that achievement is what really matters. When in the rat race, I do indeed need to exercise my strengths to succeed. This is what makes me stand out and win the competition. But what if winning is not my main concern or objective?

Also, is it really right that working on weaknesses is irrelevant? If you are a talented tennis player with an excellent forehand and a weak backhand, should you just ignore the latter? And what happens if you have a weakness in a domain that you value? Say, for example, you have many strengths related to knowledge, but are rather bad in terms of humanity and love. Yet, you may still want to develop a deep, loving relationship. Should you just focus on playing to your strengths?

In some way, the strengths theory contradicts another well-evidenced positive psychology theory, that of *mindsets* (Dweck, 2006). Developed and substantiated by Carol Dweck, the theory postulates that believing that one's capacities are fixed at birth, even at a very high level, invariably leads to a 'helplessness' response in the face of failure and abandoning efforts when the goal turns out to be harder than expected to achieve. Just to make it more tangible, if I believe I am clever, but then come across a mathematical task I can't solve, this must mean I am not clever enough, so what's the point in trying? This so-called *fixed mindset* is contrasted with the *growth/flexible mindset*, which fundamentally sees people as malleable, open and able to change through the effort they invest. Such people respond to failure with an attitude of mastery and simply keep trying instead of thinking they are not good enough. So another problem with a strengths movement is the potential 'fixing' of the strengths, seeing them as something inborn and therefore opening them up to all the problems of a fixed mindset. Out of all strengths theorists, Linley appears to be the only one who accounts for this problem by stating that 'our strengths are not fixed at birth, but instead emerge and develop and evolve over the course of our life and through the different situations we experience' (Linley, 2011).

Finally, I wonder what happens if one over-develops one's strengths? Extreme creativity can turn into chaos; curiosity, bravery and optimism can lead to recklessness; persistence, if pushed, may end up in stubbornness; kindness can be overbearing, and citizenship can lead to nationalism and religious fanaticism. Again, to be fair, Realise2 does acknowledge this danger, by suggesting that the use of strengths is calibrated, akin to using a volume control button (Linley et al., 2010). So the answer, as so often, seems to be one of moderation and balance.

Note

1 I personally tend to agree with them with regard to the first assumption, but disagree as far as the second is concerned. A simple mathematical representation of strengths and weaknesses as either above or below zero would suggest

that if one were to bring their −5 quality (weakness) to +10, the growth would be greater than if +5 quality (strength) was developed to +10.

Further reading

Dweck, C. (2006). *Mindset: The new psychology of success*. New York: Random House.

Linley, A., Willars, J., & Biswas-Diener, R. (2010). *The strengths book*. Coventry: CAPP Press.

Chapter Twelve
Love

One of the fundamental characteristics of humanity is the 'need to belong'. Self-determination theory (Chapter 6) calls it relatedness – the need to have close and secure human connections. When this need is satisfied, we experience positive emotions and feelings, while long-lasting periods of loneliness are often characterized by negative affect and dissatisfaction (Berscheid, 2003).

The need to belong co-exists with another basic need – for expansion of boundaries of the self. This self-expansion can be achieved through several means, including material possessions, money, power, influence and love. Love enables a rapid (thus immensely pleasurable) transition from the existential isolation of 'me' and 'you' to the subjective fusion experienced as 'us' (Aron & Aron, 1996).

Positive psychology places a lot of emphasis on interpersonal connections. Here are some relevant facts. Relationships, especially intimate ones, are considered the best predictors of happiness: 40 per cent of married people see themselves as 'very happy', compared with 23 per cent of never-married individuals. Many of the valued strengths (love, kindness, emotional intelligence, forgiveness, teamwork, etc.) are of an interpersonal nature. Women in stable relationships ovulate more regularly and reach menopause later than other women. Children of stable marriages do better in terms of education, psychological health and relationships than children of any other arrangements (Seligman, 2002).

How we presently conceive of love is a recent phenomenon (although undoubtedly the core experience is 'as old as time'). In the Middle Ages, for example, the normal form of love was courtly love – a ritualistic, intensely passionate experience, shared by two people usually not married to each other (which means that most of the time love was left unsatisfied). In the Western world, love and marriage did not tend to co-exist until the eighteenth century. Nowadays, being and remaining in love are usually seen as necessary factors for a lasting marriage. Taken that passionate love is often short-lived, it's no wonder that intimate relationships frequently suffer from lack of longevity. The current tendency is towards promoting friendship as a basis of love that can withstand time (Hendrick & Hendrick, 2002).

Models of love

There are several models and conceptions of love, only some of which are discussed below. They were chosen either because of their popularity in positive psychology, or because of their substantial theoretical and/or empirical history.

Attachment theory

Attachment theory is often advocated as an overarching framework for human relationships, partly because it attempts to explain relationships in both childhood and adulthood, partly because it has served as a research basis for more studies than any other love/relationship theory.

A fundamental concept of this theory is an inborn attachment system in infants that functions to regulate proximity to the caregiver and thus increases survival (Peterson & Seligman, 2004). A typical one-year-old usually plays happily in the presence of his mother, but if she moves or goes away, he will get upset and start crying in order to re-establish proximity. While this is a normal pattern of infant behaviour, psychologists have discovered that not all children exhibit the same patterns of attachment. They have used a famous technique, called the Strange

Situation Test, to reveal the attachment bond between a mother and child. During this test, a one-year-old child is left in a room with a friendly stranger on two occasions, while his mother vacates the room. The pattern of attachment is discerned from the child's reaction upon reunion with his or her mother. *Securely* attached children are upset when their mother leaves, but are easily soothed by her upon her return. Other children are more anxious and unusually clingy. They are very distressed by the separation, but resist the mother's attempts to provide comfort on her return and continue crying for a prolonged period of time. This pattern is called *ambivalent* attachment. The third group of children appear to be little affected by the absence of their mother on the surface (although all physiological indicators show that they are in distress), and actively avoid contact on her return (by averting their gaze, ignoring her invitations to play, etc.). This attachment pattern is *avoidant.*

You may wonder what the reactions of one-year-old babies have got to do with love. What many researchers show is that the pattern of attachment in childhood can predict the pattern of attachment in adulthood. Secure children grow into *autonomous* adults, ambivalent children into *preoccupied* ones, and avoidant children into *dismissive* ones. Interestingly, infants on the Strange Situation Test usually show a corresponding pattern to their parents (e.g. autonomous adults have secure children, etc.). Moreover, the patterns of attachment in adulthood may influence how people approach and experience romantic relationships.

- *Autonomous* adults find it quite easy to get close to others, are trusting and trustworthy, and are comfortable with mutual co-dependence. The autonomous attachment style is associated with using productive conflict resolution strategies, higher self-esteem, less depression and less likelihood of divorce (Peterson & Seligman, 2004).
- *Anxious/preoccupied* adults want to get very close to another person in a romantic relationship, almost merge with them, which can

scare many people away. They often worry that their partner does not love them enough.

• *Avoidant/dismissive* adults are the opposite of the previous group. They are quite uncomfortable getting close to other people and find it hard to trust or depend on them. They value independence, emotional distance and withdraw easily.

Recent experimental evidence provides further validity to the adult attachment theory. Accepting your partner's needs for dependence helps them to be more independent, enabling engagement in independent exploration, achievement of independent goals, feelings of independence, self-reliance, self-confidence and capability. Even more importantly, a partner's acceptance of dependence predicts increases in the recipient's independent functioning six months later. Put simply, accepting dependence promotes independence. Just as a mother's acceptance of her baby's dependence helps the baby to separate on their own terms, accepting the dependence of adults helps them feel secure enough to start exploring the world on their own. So when another adult human being comes clinging to you, think twice before rejecting this seemingly infantile behaviour.

Triangular theory of love

The triangular theory of love was developed by the same psychologist, Robert Sternberg, who proposed the balanced theory of wisdom. Beautifully written, his book *The Triangle of Love: Intimacy, Passion, Commitment* (1988), starts with a rather pessimistic observation that passionate love begins at such a height that wherever it goes afterwards, it can only be down. This is unless something else is in play. Sternberg believes that love is a mix of intimacy, passion and commitment. Intimacy involves self-disclosure, sharing emotions and thoughts with one's partner. Passion is about erotic and sexual interest and desire. Making a decision to stay with this particular partner is expressed as commitment.

Each of these parameters may be well- or under-developed in any given relationship, giving rise to eight types of love. If all three components are absent, this signals *non-love*, a relationship based on intimacy only is a *friendship*, one on passion *infatuation* (often felt as love at first sight), and on commitment *empty love* (all that is frequently left after the passion has gone). A mix of intimacy and commitment gives rise to *compassionate love*, of passion and commitment to *fatuous love*, of intimacy and passion to *romantic love*. The presence of all three indicates *consummate love*. Sternberg believes that a relationship based on a single element is less likely to survive than one that is based on two or more. Needless to say, consummate love is the relationship ideal that only few achieve, and even fewer manage to maintain.

Love styles

Many researchers on love distinguish between six different types or styles of love. Some of them are based on and vaguely correspond to the philosophical conceptions of love (Compte-Sponville, 2004):

- *Mania* is, as the name suggests, love that is somewhat manic and a bit abnormal. 'I want you but I fear getting close' or 'I want you and I hate you' could be typical expressions of it. This style of loving is often characterized by stormy outbursts, intense arguments, walk-outs, explosions of jealousy and intense reconciliations (usually accompanied by passionate sexual exchanges).
- *Ludus* is a game of love. It's pleasant and shallow, based not on commitment but on mutual enjoyment. The partner is not, and does not need to be, unique. This style may have glimpses of passion but without the intensity of Eros.
- *Pragma* is love based on pragmatism. One is shopping for the 'right partner', who would tick all the boxes in the checklist (e.g. good provider, potentially good father, good looking, etc.).

- *Eros* is an intense, passionate love, which idealizes the other. Eros, which is a desire to have, to possess and to retain, is similar to Sternberg's passion. Eros loving fundamentally means wanting. Because this love does not have trust or faith, it often suspects the other and can also bring unhappiness and suffering.
- *Storge* is love based on friendship. It is similar to what the Greeks called *Philia*, a joyful, happy, sharing love that involves loving another for the other's sake. To love means being happy that another exists and to wish them happiness. Sexuality and passion can be a part of it, but not the driving principle. This type of love corresponds to the compassionate love mentioned both above and below.
- *Agape* is the type of love that is selfless, welcoming and giving, primarily concerned with the other's well-being. It accepts, protects, gives of itself and does not even ask for love (or anything else) in return. In late Greek philosophy, it is love for many (who are not necessarily close) others: neighbours, friends, enemies. It closely corresponds to religious conceptions of love, and translates into English as 'charity'.

In psychology, these six types of love are independent. In philosophy, however, the main three are sequential. The primary impulse is manifested in Eros, while the endpoint is found in Agape. Philia, on the other hand, is a relatively joyful path from passion to selfless compassion. This path, however, may not be as easy as the description of Philia sounds.

Passionate and compassionate love

Many scholars make a clear distinction between these two broad types of love (Hendrick & Hendrick, 2002). *Passionate love* is equivalent to a state of infatuation; it's an intense desire for another person, which can be completely involving. It is often characterized by excitement, moments of exultation, feeling accepted, safe and even a sense of union and transcendence, but also by mood swings, anxiety, despair and jealousy. It is commonly believed that falling in love cannot be helped. However, it is usually triggered by identifying fulfilment of one's needs and desires with another person, or simply projecting one's ideal onto the other. Passionate love is temporary, because sooner or later inevitable differences between the idealized and the actual other become so prominent that they can no longer be ignored.

Compassionate love reflects a deep affection that people feel for each other. Love that begins with the uncontrollable and unpredictable fire of passion usually (provided it survives the first stage) quietens into a beautiful glow of compassion. Compassionate love may be less intense but is lasting. It can be seen to have four elements: being, doing, staying and growing with the other person (Popovic, 2005).

Being with the other refers to acceptance, care, respect (including self-respect) and mutual equality. *Doing with the other* means having shared goals or activities and mutual interests, alongside and in addition to the individual ones. Doing sometimes involves helping, comforting and protecting the other. *Staying with the other* is based on commitment between people. It is assisted by intimacy and closeness. *Growing with the other* involves transcending one's own interests and a willingness to change. It is a commonsense wisdom that everyone changes in his or her lifetime. Change therefore is an essential element of life and relationships. In a partnership, it is important that the rates and directions of change in individuals are to some extent compatible. This benefits the relationship and enhances its growth.

While passionate love and compassionate love are usually seen as sequential and even mutually exclusive, some believe that they can co-exist in a relationship (Hartfield, 1988).

Love against time

John and Julie Gottman, two acclaimed love scientists, identified the so-called 'Four Horsemen of the Apocalypse' that allow them to predict with up to 90 per cent accuracy if a couple is heading for divorce:

- *Criticism* – picking up the negative points of another, complaining, using words such as 'always' or 'never'.
- *Contempt* – taking criticism one level up by adding in hostility, mockery and disgust.
- *Defensiveness* – defending innocence, avoiding taking responsibility, whining.
- *Stonewalling* – withdrawal from the conversation to the extent it is not clear whether the person is listening at all.

On the other hand, behaving like good friends, with lots of respect, affection and empathy, and handling conflicts in gentle and positive ways are reliable signs of a long-lasting marriage (Gottman & Levenson, 2002).

Tips & Tools
Ten good ways to destroy a relationship:

1. Criticize your partner rather than his actions.
2. Display your contempt regularly (through insults, hostile humour and mockery).
3. Attempt to control your partner.
4. Get defensive at every opportunity.
5. Take your partner for granted.
6. Don't show interest in your partner and what she is doing.
7. Avoid communication by distancing yourself physically or emotionally.
8. Jump straight away into the deep end of an argument.
9. Make sure the TV is on when your partner comes home.
10. Adopt strong traditional roles, even if one of you believes in equality.

Minding model

Certain objective factors are associated with marital satisfaction (Newman & Newman, 1991), including: high level of education, good socio-economic status, similarity of interests and levels of intelligence, being in the beginning or a late stage of family cycle (before and after children), sexual compatibility and later marriage for women.

Often, however, not much can be done to change objective circumstances (if you already have young children, you can't reverse it or fast forward their development), so the key to maintaining a relationship is your own and your partner's effort and persistence. The so-called *minding model* of relationship development focuses not so much on what love consists of, as on how to make it last and grow (Harvey et al., 2004). It identifies five specific components of successful relationships:

- *Knowing and being known* is about behaviour aimed at learning about each other. It involves questioning and disclosing, knowing about thoughts, feelings, attitudes and past history. What is essential here is a desire to understand the other, rather than just aiming at self-expression. This knowledge, of course, can facilitate the relationship (e.g. he washes up because he knows that his partner hates doing it). However, knowing becomes more challenging as the relationship progresses, because we tend to take what another is saying for granted, thinking that we *already* know.
- *Attributions* are the explanations that we make about our partner's behaviour. What works well is attributing positive behaviour to the character and intentions of the partner ('He finished work earlier to spend time with me'), and attributing negative behaviour to external circumstances (e.g. traffic jam, heavy day at work), unless proven wrong.
- *Acceptance and respect* are necessary even (or, perhaps, especially) in an argument: aim to listen to each other respectfully, accept the other's responses and work out compromises. It's perfectly healthy

to complain about something specific, but not to criticize the whole person. Well-minding couples do not allow negativity to become habitual. They use rewards rather than punishments in arguments, and lots of validation in daily life (Seligman, 2002). Researchers find that happy couples have a ratio of negative to positive exchanges of one to five (Gottman, 1993).

* *Reciprocity* relates to a sense of equality, when one's gains are approximately equal to one's investments. A relationship is working well when nobody is taken advantage of. Distribution of housework can be an example. While it is perfectly okay to take certain roles (for convenience), doing so has to involve respect, recognition and appreciation.

* *Continuity*. Minding is a process rather than a final destination, thus it requires time and continuity. This process never stops, because a relationship is always developing, adjusting to new information, changes in personalities and life cycles.

Many argue that successful couples tend to maintain positive illusions about each other (Seligman, 2002). They not only see in their partners what their own friends don't, they even explain things that are plainly wrong in positive terms (for example, stubbornness can be interpreted as strong beliefs, excessive jealousy as deep love, and so on). Minding theorists disagree with this position, by promoting a strong reality orientation. They believe that the focus on the relationship requires a dialogue about some things that may be painful and one would rather avoid. Addressing faults contributes to the quality of the relationship (Harvey et al., 2004).

While some pain is probably inevitable in all relationships (whether it is an affair, pressures of work and/or family, etc.), successful couples are usually the ones who are able to forgive. *Forgiveness* or letting go of grudges is an important strength for building good relationships and is closely related to empathy or an ability to understand the feelings of others. Seligman thinks that the value of forgiveness lies in acknowledging that someone did you wrong but then removing the 'sting'. In fact, forgiveness can even transform the experience. There are many empirically validated studies that document the positive effects of forgiveness, including less anger, more optimism and better health (Seligman, 2002). The other essential relationship skill is *gratitude*, or not taking your partner for granted. The expression of gratitude is associated with happiness, well-being, physical exercise, life satisfaction, optimism, enthusiasm and love, with gratitude being a kind of meta-strategy for achieving happiness (described further in the next chapter) (Emmons, 2007).

Love, a highly desirable and pleasurable state of being, is not easy to achieve. This is not only because the right partner is hard to find, but also because maintaining and developing love requires a lot of work. I would like to finish this chapter with the words of the humanistic psychologist, Erich Fromm, from his book *The Art of Loving*, written in 1957 (but as modern now as it was then): 'Mature *love is union under the condition of preserving one's integrity*, one's individuality. *Love is an active power in man*; a power which breaks through the walls which separate man from his fellow men, which unites him with others; love makes him overcome the sense of isolation and separateness, yet it permits him to be himself, to retain his integrity. In love the paradox occurs that two beings become one and yet remain two' (Fromm, 1957/1995: 16).

Further reading

Gottman, J., & Silver, N. (2007). *The seven principles for making marriage work*. London: Orion.

Sternberg, R.J. (1988). *The triangle of love: Intimacy, passion, commitment*. New York: Basic Books.

Chapter Thirteen
Positive Psychology Interventions

This chapter is for those occasionally visited by a fleeting thought along the lines of 'And what about me?' How can you implement some of the positive psychology findings in your own life? Since the first edition of this book, considerable progress has been made in testing relatively simple positive psychology interventions through controlled experimental studies (this is when you randomly allocate participants into two or more groups and compare the proposed intervention with another exercise intended as a placebo).

What follows may look like a shopping list for weekly groceries (rather than a party, for example, when all components are meaningfully related), but it probably represents the state of positive psychology science quite accurately. Each of the techniques below has been tested individually, rather than as part of a package. The advantage of this approach is that it allows the teasing out of the individual effects of each intervention. The disadvantage is that it does not go far enough – the testing of combinations of these techniques would surely have a greater impact than testing one at a time. Well, time will probably tell. To spice up the chapter further, I have also added a few more interventions that are definitely 'positive', but are still queuing for their turn for empirical validation.

Evidence-based interventions

Three good things

Probably the most powerful of all positive psychology techniques, different variants of this exercise have been investigated (Sheldon & Lyubomirsky, 2004; Seligman et al., 2005), always with interesting results. It has been found to increase happiness and decrease depressive symptoms for up to six months (Seligman et al., 2005). However, this does not mean that after the six months the effects had worn off, but simply that the participants were not followed beyond this point.

The instructions are fairly straightforward. Every night for a week, look back at your day just before you go to bed and think of three things that went well for you during the day. Write them down and reflect on your role in them. There are three caveats. Writing down is important as it helps you to focus on the events. Reflecting on your own role is no less essential, as it contributes to your sense of perceived control, which, in turn, has an impact on well-being. Your role in some of these events may not always appear obvious to you – if the sky was beautiful and blue today, what did you have to do with it? Well, 'notice' it is one possible answer. Finally, the timing of this exercise is significant – either stick to it for one week, or try it once a week for six weeks. Studies have shown that the well-being of those who carried it out three times a week for six weeks actually decreased slightly, which suggests that there is such a thing as too much (Sheldon & Lyubomirsky, 2004)! This finding co-exists with the fact that people who continue 'counting their blessings' occasionally after the intervention week demonstrate the best outcomes. The most likely conclusion is that it is important to notice the good things in life now and then, yet not allow this practice to become a chore.

If at this point you are feeling that I have suddenly lost all my critical capacities and slipped into a marshland of over-claiming (i.e. 'the most powerful'), I would urge you not to jump to that conclusion. When the data first came out and I began to introduce this exercise to my students, I was rather embarrassed by its simplicity. Eventually, I decided to try it out on myself. The first night it took me about half-an-hour to remember one good thing, though I could remember perfectly everything that I did wrong during a presentation, the number of emails I did not answer and all the other projects I was late with. On the second night, I suddenly realized why my partner gets so upset when I come home from work and ask him why the kitchen surfaces are untidy before even taking my coat off. On the third night . . . well, you get the point.

A gratitude visit

If your happiness needs an immediate boost, try this intervention (Seligman et al., 2005). I have to warn you that the boost will not necessarily last, and six months down the road you are likely to be where you started, but that does not mean that momentary well-being should be shunned.

Think of a person you feel grateful to for something that they have done for you in the past. Pick up a piece of paper – or your laptop – and write a letter to them, describing what they did and what effect it had on you and your life. Once you have finished, give this person a ring and arrange to meet them, preferably in their house. When you meet, stand or sit in front of them and read your letter out loud.

When teaching, I usually pause once I reach the end of this exercise and nine times out of ten the audience is awash with giggling. A note of clarification – most of the time I present to British or European audiences. I know from experience that this does not happen with American ones. The usual moral dilemmas frequently arise, such as whom this exercise is really for and if there is something strange in saying 'thank you' to someone else in order to feel better oneself. Though not as robust empirically, one way of solving these dilemmas is to send the letter. You may miss the tears, but the message will be got across.

Random acts of kindness

As the name suggests, this intervention is about doing something good for another human being. This may be large or small, but the act needs to benefit them in some way. Options can range from donating blood to taking your neighbour's dog for a walk, from visiting your elderly aunt to giving someone a free tube ticket. In our age of social networking sites, the opportunities for small touches are practically endless. One of my students sent all of her friends on Facebook a so-called Growing Gift – a flower that is hidden at first but comes to bloom within a few days.

Not only do random acts of kindness make the recipient feel better, they also make the giver happier, especially if several acts are carried out on the same day. So here again, optimal timing becomes critical. It is also important to vary these acts so that they remain fresh and meaningful (Lyubomirsky, 2008).

Active-constructive responding

If you have begun to suspect that all positive psychology interventions stem from the Judeo-Christian tradition, the next one, though still other-oriented, will not fit the bill quite so well.

Shelly Gable and her colleagues concluded that what distinguishes good relationships from poor ones is not how partners react to problems, but how they welcome the good news in each other's lives (Gable et al., 2004). There are a number of ways in which we can react to our partner getting promoted, for example. Very often, we adopt a passive-constructive strategy: we acknowledge their success – 'well done, dear!' – and then move on. At times, good news can even trigger nega-tive emotional reactions in us, such as jealousy, envy, anger or anxiety, and we may react in an unconstructive manner. An example of an active-destructive response could be: 'Have you thought of all the extra time you would have to spend at work and not with your family?' A passive-destructive strategy would be to undermine someone's success by simply ignoring it, pretending it didn't happen: 'Is dinner ready?' Research shows that relationships that favour all of the above strategies are less close, supportive and trusting (Lyubomirsky, 2008).

So how can we respond to good news in an active-constructive way? First, we should try to understand what happened – through paying close attention to the person, listening, asking questions, being interested and enthusiastic. The second stage is celebration and capitalizing on the success – open a bottle of champagne, call your close relatives and friends to tell them the news, do something together with your loved one that you always wanted to, but never got around to.

Identifying signature strengths

In the 'Tips and Tools' box in Chapter 11 (see p. 114), I suggested a quick way of identifying your so-called signature strengths by using the list in Table 11.1. Now visit www.authentichappiness.org and take the 40-minute long VIA survey. At the end, it will help you to identify your top strengths. Print out or write down the feedback you receive about your signature strengths. Try to use these strengths more often during the following week and notice how this makes you feel. This exercise won't make you happy for ever, but it can improve your mood quite dramatically in the short term (Seligman et al., 2005).

Using your strengths in a new way

This exercise goes one step further than the previous one, which is probably why its effects are far more lasting (Seligman et al., 2005). Follow the instructions above to identify your signature strengths. Then, every day for the next seven days, use one of your top five strengths in a way that you have not done so before. It can be in a new setting or with a new person – the choice is yours. If one of your signature strengths is love of learning, you may choose to spend a couple of hours researching a topic that always interested you in some way. If it is appreciation of beauty and excellence, you might enjoy spending your lunch hour visiting a museum [you may also be interested to know that a half-hour museum visit dramatically reduces the concentration of the stress hormone cortisol in your body (Clow & Fredhoi, 2006)]. Social intelligence may be used to make your customers' day, while kindness can also be applied to oneself.

This intervention is not as straightforward as it sounds. Unless your top strength is creativity, coming up with new ideas may be tough. After all, you are already using your strengths, so what else can you do with them? One way around this problem is to pair up with someone else engaged in the same exercise – he or she can be your 'strength buddy'. No specific tips here, just the old principle that two heads may be better than one.

Savouring

Do you linger over coffee or tea in the morning, enjoying the aroma even before your first sip, and then feel the hot liquid warming you from within? Or do you mindlessly sip your coffee and eat your breakfast while busily attending to some other task? Today, when you are having your cuppa, try to get fully immersed in this experience: try not to think, just sense.

It is this phenomenon that positive psychologists call savouring. According to Bryant and Veroff (2007: 2), 'people have capacities to attend, appreciate and enhance the positive experiences in their lives'.

Noticing and savouring life's small and big positive occurrences is a powerful tool for increasing one's overall well-being. We can find them in our daily lives or intentionally focus on specific activities. Positive psychologists have identified several techniques that promote savouring, some of which are detailed below:

- *Sharing with others.* You can seek out others to share the experience and tell others how much you value the moment. This is probably the single best way to savour pleasure.

- *Memory-building.* Take mental photographs of the event and reminisce about it later.
- *Self-congratulation.* Do not be afraid of pride. Tell yourself how impressed others are and remember how long you've waited for this to happen.
- *Sharpening perceptions.* Focus on certain elements of an immediate experience and block out all others.
- *Absorption.* Let yourself get totally immersed and try not to think, just sense.

It's important to emphasize that savouring is not exactly the same as mindfulness because it does not imply openness to all inner and outer stimuli, and focuses solely on those generating positive affect. However, practising mindfulness can also be considered a positive intervention associated with decreased depression, as well as positive effects on happiness, physiology and cognitive abilities.

Exercise

Returning to age-old wisdom, the next intervention on the list is exercise. Even though I am sure that you already know that physical activity is important, I chose to include this intervention to discuss just how important it is for a good life.

Do you know, for example, that exercise reduces anxiety and stress, the risk of hypertension, of type 2 diabetes, heart disease, insomnia, obesity and probability of dementia? That it improves not only physical but also cognitive functioning? That a bit of exercise can double muscle strength in frail adults of 87 years of age? Even more, psychological research demonstrates that exercise may be the most reliable happiness booster of all activities (Lyubomirsky, 2008).

Tal Ben-Shahar, one of the most popular lecturers at Harvard University whose positive psychology classes attract 1400 students each semester, often notes that not exercising is like taking depressants. And here is why. A famous study compared three groups of depressed patients. The first group was prescribed anti-depressants, the second group aerobic exercise, and the third a combination of the two. Independently of the treatment regime, most patients had improved four months after taking part. Unexpected results, however, were observed six months down the road, when 38 per cent of responders in the first group (anti-depressants only) relapsed into depression, as did 31 per cent of those in the combination treatment, whereas only 9 per cent of those in the exercise-only group became depressed again (Babyak et al., 2000).

Best possible self

Once you have tried the here and now, why not reach for the there and back? The next intervention to be considered is about developing a future representation of oneself, while the one that concludes the list is about engaging with good memories.

Consider a desired future image of yourself – imagine that everything has gone the way you hoped for, that you have achieved what you aimed for, that your best potentials have come to be realized. Write about and vividly imagine yourself in that future and continue engaging with this exercise for the course of four weeks. This exercise enhances optimism and helps to achieve a better integration between one's priorities and goals, which is why it is hardly surprising that an increase in happiness follows.

An interesting caveat, however, is that this intervention does need to rely on the future projection to be successful. Thinking and writing about the time when you were at your best in the past increases happiness only slightly, with the changes failing to reach a level of significance (Seligman et al., 2005).

Positive reminiscence

Have you ever thought that picking up a photo album is, in itself, a positive intervention? This action seems almost too simple to deserve this status. Well, it may be not as simple as it sounds. It makes both theoretical and empirical sense that remembering some happy times from the past ought to enhance one's well-being. But is all remembering good, or are there better and worse ways to remember? For example, should one consider why and how a positive experience had occurred or just let one's memory run wild?

One study asked its participants to set aside ten minutes twice a day for a week to engage with their positive memories. In one condition, they were asked to reflect on one of their memories by allowing the associated images to come to mind. The other, memorabilia, group was asked to focus on an object associated with their good memories. Unsurprisingly, both groups experienced an increase in their positive feelings. Saying that, those asked to simply imagine their memories had seen their memories more vividly and experienced more positive emotions (Bryant et al., 2005). Similarly, Sonia Lyubomirsky (2008) has shown that analysing one's past does little to enhance happiness, while replaying or reliving positive life events as though rewinding a videotape enhances joy. Yet again, the devil seems to be in the detail rather than in the activity itself!

Some untested interventions

It takes time to work out the ingredients of the good life. Although to date only about a dozen positive psychology interventions have been tested, there are hundreds of exercises and techniques aimed at increasing positive functioning that can be found in self-help books, neuro-linguistic programming (NLP) manuals and popular psychology literature. Do they work? The most probable answer is that a substantial proportion of them do, we just don't know which ones they are, nor do we know under what conditions these techniques produce desired outcomes. I trust that it is only a matter of time until these questions are answered, but for the time being I have decided to include six of my favourite interventions that fall into this category. All have a substantive theoretical base (i.e. we can put together a convincing argument for why they should work), but they have not been tested in controlled studies.

A beautiful day together

Design a beautiful day for yourself and someone else – your partner, or a close friend. Include activities that both of you would find highly enjoyable, as well as those that are really important for each of you. Take into consideration the strengths of both of you when choosing activities. Spend time planning what you would do from first thing in the morning until bedtime. Decide when you are going to make the day happen, taking into account other demands on your time. Finally, go ahead and live the day out, savouring your chosen activities and each other's company.

Plugged-in

Barbara Fredrickson describes a ritual she performs with her husband of asking to be 'plugged in' when she needs a good hug. The instructions are that the hug should be front-to-front and last closer to a minute than to a second (Fredrickson, 2009). When reading her book, *Positivity*, I realized that I tend to do exactly the same with my own husband and it really does help. Now asking for a hug has a name and can therefore qualify as an intervention!

A gift of time

We may be good at remembering someone's birthdays, buying Christmas gifts or even making unexpected surprises. This exercise suggests going beyond our normal activities and giving someone the greatest gift of all – your time. It may be just an hour or the whole day. They can make their own choices about how to use it. Your aunt may just want to spend this time talking about your family; your neighbour may prefer to do some gardening together; your kids may choose to play hide-and-seek.

Your life summary

Imagine that one day, long after you have passed away, one of your grandchildren asks about you and your life. How would you want to be remembered and described? Write a one-page summary of your life as you would like it to be known to your grandchild. Include a description of your values, personal characteristics and your contribution to humanity. Put this summary aside for a few days and then come back to it. What did you include in your summary and what did you omit? What changes might you make in your life so that this life summary might one day be an accurate reflection of your life?[1]

Worry reduction

This exercise comes from an approach known as Quality of Life Therapy (Frisch, 2006), although it has also been mentioned in other sources (Popovic, 2005). Although it has been tested as a package with medical patients, most of its techniques have not been evaluated individually. This intervention is useful for those who find that they may be spending too much time on worrying. We cannot will ourselves not to worry, so it can easily become an unproductive pattern. Habitual worriers may find relief if they allocate a limited period (e.g. fifteen or thirty minutes) every day for worrying that is to occur at the same time and in the same place, and postpone any worrying until then.

Three-question process

This exercise, also entitled the Meaning, Pleasure, Strengths (MPS) Process, was outlined by Tal Ben-Shahar (2007) in his book *Happier*. In a nutshell, it involves answering three questions:

- What gives me meaning?
- What gives me pleasure?
- What are my strengths?

These are straightforward questions, yet how often do we actually ask them of ourselves? Spend some time reflecting on these questions; avoid jumping to conclusions too quickly.

The next step involves discovering where and how the answers you come up with overlap. What activities would bring you both meaning and pleasure, while using what you are good at? How can you use the MPS process further to help you make important decisions in your life? There is a danger that the interventions above may appear too simplistic. Think about yourself well, do what you are good at, focus on the good aspects of your life and be nice to others. In short, be more positive and your life will be better. Well, this is hardly surprising considering that most of these techniques enhance hedonic rather than eudaimonic well-being.

Note

1 Martin Seligman, personal communication.

Further reading

Lyubomirsky, S. (2008). *The HOW of happiness*. London: Sphere.

Chapter Fourteen
Putting it into Practice

Theory can be of little use unless it is put into practice. Also, it is only practice that allows us to determine whether the theory is right or wrong. Positive psychology is now being increasingly applied in different domains, the most notable of which are one-to-one work with clients, education and business.

Positive psychology and one-to-one practices

'A new kid on the block', *coaching* is a natural ally of positive psychology. It is a relatively new phenomenon, which has exploded in popularity since the 1980s (Kauffman & Scoular, 2004). Starting out as executive coaching, focused on high flyers whose companies could afford to pay for their development, it is now available for everyone (not only those who are already wealthy and successful) under the name of 'life coaching'. Coaching aims to produce fast personality changes through the setting and acquisition of goals. It is explicitly concerned with the promotion of well-being and performance (Palmer & Whybrow, 2005), something that positive psychology takes an active interest in. Despite similarities in the name, executive and life coaching have little to do with sport coaching, aimed at training professional sportspeople.

In recent years, a highly successful partnership has been formed between coaching and positive psychology. Coaching benefits from positive psychology, because the latter offers a much needed theoretical and research base. Positive psychology, on the other hand, finds that coaching can serve as a good soundboard to its scholarly ideas. Today, there are several courses on coaching and positive psychology, including a Master's degree at the University of Pennsylvania.

Positive psychology and coaching both claim that attention should be redirected from 'fixing' the client, or looking for signs of pathology (which, supposedly, is a job of therapists), to finding what is right with the person and working on enhancing it. Thus, coaching is intended to work on the construction of the client's skill base and development of their unrecognized talents and resources. In addition to identifying clients' strengths, it can be employed to evaluate how well such strengths are being utilized in the workplace and to help create further opportunities for their use. Rather than focusing on improving weaknesses, which can take enormous efforts, this idea centres on utilizing strengths to the maximum and compensating for existing weaknesses through, for example, complementary partnering or strengths-matched teams (Linley & Harrington, 2006).

Despite its growing popularity, coaching is not without its problems, which include the lack of a conceptual and evaluative base, the briefness of coaching training courses, manufacturing half-baked professionals, a lack of regulations and ethical standards, and a 'throw it all in' approach to practice, which often leads to superficiality (Peltier, 2001). Moreover, focusing on goals and actions often offers nothing but a short-term solution, if underlying issues and dilemmas are left unexamined and unresolved. Does this mean that a bit of a 'negative' approach may not only be useful, but even necessary for workable goals and lasting improvement in performance? And if the answer is 'yes', is coaching really that different from its predecessors, counselling and psychotherapy? To answer these questions, let us look at the relationships between coaching and other types of one-to-one practices in more detail.

Coaching and therapy – differences and similarities

'Negative psychology' or 'psychology as usual' made the biggest contribution to the world through its brainchild – therapy. Today, fourteen psychological disorders, previously considered untreatable, can be successfully helped by therapeutic interventions. Therapy comes in many shapes, colours and sizes. First, we can distinguish between *counselling* and *psychotherapy*, although practitioners themselves find it hard to discern what differentiates them and often treat them as one profession in practice. Then, there are many different types of therapy: behavioural therapy (changing behaviour will change the way you think), cognitive-behavioural therapy (reprogramme your thinking and take actions), psychoanalysis (fathered by Freud), psychodynamic therapy (mothered by Freud's daughter), Gestalt therapy (the way of becoming whole), existential therapy (dealing with the human condition), client-centred therapy (client knows best), transactional analysis (integrating the child-parent-adult in yourself), integrative therapy (taking the best bits from everywhere and putting them together into a coherent new framework) and many others. The choice on offer is really too much for any normal, non-informed (in this area) person, which is why it is usually determined by chance and 'clicking' with a particular therapist. Generally speaking, therapy is a highly successful endeavour; although only about 10–15 per cent of its success can be attributed to the type of therapeutic intervention (Lambery & Barley, 2002). Nevertheless, therapy is generally associated with deficiency, implying that there is something wrong with a 'patient' and that there is a need for remedial intervention. This association with 'fixing' drives away many potential clients and creates a niche for coaches.

Whether the line between therapy and coaching is clear-cut (or should be there at all) is an open question. Not surprisingly, in the fight for the place under the sun, coaching tries to emphasize the differences between itself and its sister professions, while deliberately ignoring similarities (Bachkirova & Coz, 2004). For example, it is often emphasized that therapists take a reactive role, whereas coaches take a more proactive role (Whitmore, 1997). This is not true for many behavioural and cognitive-behavioural therapists, who are very proactive in their approach. Counselling, psychotherapy and coaching are also often artificially separated by temporal perspective (apparently, counselling and psychotherapy deal with the past, coaching with the present and future), or by specifying a client group (working with clinically pathological vs. the normal population, which are themselves fuzzy and controversial terms). A remedial aim of therapy is sometimes contrasted with the performance improvement objective of coaching (Carroll, 2003). However, many counsellors do developmental work and even draw on positive psychology principles (Worsley & Joseph, 2005). The truth is that all these practices rely heavily on similar skills and in reality overlap to a large extent.

With boundaries between therapy and coaching rather loosely drawn, there are some attempts to integrate these approaches. Few clients nowadays are interested in lengthy therapy that is supposed to reveal some hidden parts of themselves, with little effect in real life. On the other hand, focusing just on goals and actions, without challenging preconceptions and resolving internal hindering conflicts, can be counterproductive. There is a lot of value in the emphasis on developing the positive, as long as it is not at the expense of simply ignoring the negative.

An approach that I have helped to develop, *personal consultancy*, is such an attempt to create a new, integrative method of working one-to-one with clients. Offering a four-stage model (authentic listening, rebalancing, generating, supporting), it combines the strengths of both counselling and coaching. It allows clients to explore their depths and also to make constructive, practical changes through setting goals and undertaking actions. Personal consultancy thus integrates positive and mainstream psychology in practice (Popovic & Boniwell, 2007).

Positive psychology coaching

What, then, is positive psychology coaching? Positive psychology coaching (PPC) is a scientifically rooted approach to helping clients increase well-being, enhance and apply strengths, improve performance, and achieve valued goals. At the core of PPC is a belief in the power of science to elucidate the best approaches for positively transforming clients' lives, through reliance on the use of standardized assessment and validated interventions. Similar to co-active coaching and person-centred therapy (see below), the PPC orientation suggests that the coach view the client as 'whole', and that the coach focus on strengths, positive behaviours and purpose. These, in turn, are used as building blocks and leverage points for coachees' development and performance improvement. Put simply, PPC aims to identify assets and capabilities, find out what is going well in order to build on it, and increase positive performance and well-being as broadly defined (Kauffman et al., 2009). There are a couple of 'how to' manuals for PPC, the best of which (in my view) are listed at the end of the chapter.

Positive therapy

As mentioned already, most counselling and psychotherapy approaches have traditionally focused on problems and are often perceived as stigmatizing and pathologizing. However, some types of counselling and psychotherapy can be seen to be more about promoting well-being and integration, and therefore working within a positive rather than medical model. This is the basic premise of a recent book *Positive Therapy*, which proposes that several therapeutic approaches can be integrated into positive therapy, as they offer useful models and techniques for developing strengths and resources, promoting growth and well-being (Joseph & Linley, 2007). So let's consider some of these in turn.

The *person-centred approach* provides a positive starting point with its optimistic view of the person and the potential for growth and fulfilment. Developed by a humanistic psychologist, Carl Rogers, it postulates that the client is the expert in their own life and views the therapist–client relationship (based on empathy, congruence and positive unconditional regard) as the key to successful therapy. It further talks of an actualizing tendency – an inherent drive to grow, develop and maximize one's potential as the key vehicle for achieving success in therapy (Joseph & Linley, 2007).

Well-being therapy is conceptually based on Ryff's psychological well-being model, targeting environmental mastery, personal growth, purpose in life, autonomy, self-acceptance, and positive relations with others. It consists of eight group sessions with an emphasis on self-observation with a structured diary. In a way, clients simply monitor whether or not episodes of well-being occur. Episodes (or the lack thereof) are then discussed in therapy, and obstacles are targeted with more traditional techniques (e.g. refuting negative automatic thoughts). Preliminary evidence suggests the potential of this therapy for relapse prevention in mood and anxiety disorders (Fava & Ruini, 2009).

Another type of therapy, *solution-focused brief therapy*, is based on the premise that people have the ability to find their own solutions to the problems they encounter, and that the seeds of those solutions and more effective ways of living are likely to be present somewhere within the client already. The proponents of this approach think that exploring problems in depth is unlikely to be the most effective use of therapy time (which really should take as little time as possible) and base their practice on the so-called *miracle question*, which goes as follows (De Shazer et al., 2007):

1. Suppose that while you are sleeping tonight, a miracle happens . . . and the problems that brought you here are solved, just like that! But, this happens while you are sleeping, so you cannot know that it has happened. Once you wake up in the morning, how will you discover that this miracle has happened to you? (Clients should be encouraged to develop as detailed a picture as possible of the day after the miracle.)
2. How will your best friend or other people discover that this miracle happened to you?
3. When was the most recent time (perhaps days, hours, weeks) that you can remember when things were sort of like this day after the miracle?

Finally, *acceptance and commitment therapy* is another member of the positive therapy family. It is based on the premise that behaviour and emotion can exist simultaneously and independently and, as such, a person can commit to and take a positive action without first changing or eliminating feelings (while at the same time still experiencing and accepting these feeling in a mindful fashion) (Hayes et al., 1999).

Positive psychology and education

Several education programmes have been developed within the field of positive psychology. The vast majority of these programmes reflect the main scientific topics of interest of their authors. For example, Sternberg (see Chapter 9) developed the *Wisdom Curriculum*, in which the intellectual and moral development of children is encouraged through the medium of mainstream subjects (Reznitskaya & Sternberg, 2004). *Bounce Back*, a school resilience programme devised by two Australian psychologists, McGrath and Noble, is a highly practical, teacher-friendly approach that also integrates resilience principles into mainstream subjects (McGrath & Noble, 2003). A number of projects accentuating hope in schoolchildren include *Making Hope Happen* and *Making Hope Happen for Kids* (Lopez et al., 2004). A *strengths-based development* programme, developed by the Gallup Foundation, has been found to significantly improve academic performance (Hodges & Clifton, 2004). *Emotional Intelligence* has been widely used as an umbrella concept for various programmes around social and emotional learning, the most successful of which are *Self Science* and *The South Africa Emotional Intelligence Curriculum* (Salovey et al., 2004). Some of the programmes, such as *Going for the Goal* which teaches adolescents the skills of positive goal setting and facilitation of goal attainment, have been carried out on a very large scale (Danish, 1996).

The Penn Resiliency Programme (PRP) is a schools-based intervention curriculum designed to increase resilience and promote optimism, adaptive coping skills and effective problem-solving through the application of the principles of cognitive-behavioural therapy to normal populations. Based on the seven 'learnable' skills of resilience, the programme teaches children: how to identify their feelings; tolerance of ambiguity; the optimistic explanatory style; how to analyse causes of problems; empathy; self-efficacy; and how to reach out or try new things. The PRP, therefore, educates adolescents to challenge a habitual pessimistic explanatory style by looking at the evidence and considering what is realistic, while avoiding unrealistic optimism.

The PRP has been developed and researched for over sixteen years and consequently has acquired a solid evidence base (Reivich et al., 2005). This evidence suggests that it prevents both depression and anxiety and has long-lasting effects. A meta-analysis of seventeen controlled evaluations of the programme found participants reported fewer depressive symptoms up to one year after the programme compared with young people who received no intervention (Brunwasser et al., 2009). However, the Penn Resilience Programme is essentially preventative in nature with the expressed aim of reducing depression among teenagers. For students whose future functioning is more positive, the programme is beneficial; however, it is difficult to ascertain whether it is beneficial for students not at risk of depression.

These programmes move away from the traditional schooling about things 'out there' and focus on students themselves, their personal competences and experiences. However, most of these programmes have been developed and implemented outside of Europe.

In the UK, the SPARK *Resilience Programme* is a new addition to the world of preventative positive education. Developed for and piloted in deprived neighbourhoods of East London, the programme builds on research findings from four relevant fields of study: cognitive-behavioural therapy, resilience, post-traumatic growth and positive psychology. Organized around the SPARK acronym, it teaches students to break simple and complex situations into manageable components of a Situation, Autopilot, Perception, Reaction and Knowledge. Through the use of hypothetical scenarios informed by consultations with students in pilot schools, students learn how an everyday Situation can trigger in them an Autopilot (feelings and emotions). These Autopilots vary for different people and different circumstances because of the unique way we Perceive these Situations. We then React to the Situation and learn something from it – that is, we acquire Knowledge about the way we are, or others are, or the world is. To help students understand these concepts, they are introduced to 'parrots of perception' – imaginary creatures representing common distortions of human cognition and thinking. The programme teaches students how to challenge their interpretation of any life situation and consider other alternatives by putting their parrots 'on trial', understanding their automatic emotional responses and learning to control their non-constructive behavioural reactions. In addition, they are introduced to the skills of assertiveness and problem-solving, and are helped to build their 'resilience muscles' through identifying their strengths, social support networks, sources of positive emotions and previous experiences of resilience. The statistical data analysis showed significantly higher resilience, self-esteem and self-efficacy scores in the post-assessment compared with the pre-assessment data. A marginally significant decrease was observed in depression symptoms (Boniwell et al., in prep.).

In September 2006, Wellington College – a private, co-educational school in the UK – embarked on a two-year *Skills of Well-Being* programme for its pupils (Morris, 2009). The course, designed by Ian Morris and Dr Nick Baylis, is delivered fortnightly to Years 10 and 11 (ages 14–16) with the specific aim of redressing the imbalance in modern education caused by an emphasis on exam results and measured outcomes. The ultimate outcome of the course is to give Wellington College pupils practical skills for living well that are useful, easily understood and can be applied on a daily basis. Although the course is still in its infancy, the passionate desire to deliver these skills is driving its ongoing review. This is coupled with an intention to avoid a 'myopic' approach and broaden the breadth and depth of the course to include knowledge from positive psychology, drawing on the latest evidence-based research and practical interventions. *Skills of Well-Being* has, at present, very limited scientific validation. However, it has attracted unprecedented media coverage, placing the well-being debate firmly in the heart of the British political agenda.

A further *Well-Being Curriculum* for primary and secondary schools is being piloted in the UK at present (Boniwell & Ryan, 2012). The Well-Being Curriculum is a joint project of a partnership between the Haberdashers' Aske's Academies Federation and the University of East London (UEL). The partnership has developed a comprehensive well-being curriculum based on the principles and findings of positive psychology and taught weekly to students from Year 1 to Year 13. The curriculum targets every known major predictor and correlate of well-being using individually tested interventions to enhance learning. The emphasis of the curriculum in Years 1 to 9 is on positive interventions, targeting areas that have a substantial evidence base such as happiness, positive emotions, flow, resilience, achievement, positive relationships and meaning. The emphasis in Years 10 to 13 is on positive education, enabling young people to reflect upon and make choices about their well-being and development. Pilot evaluation of the programme showed increases in various aspects of well-being (i.e. positive affect, satisfaction with friends, satisfaction with oneself) consistent with the areas targeted.

Education does not need to be limited to school settings. A number of educational programmes have been implemented in clinical group settings, thus targeting adult populations and combining therapeutic and educational practices. Mindfulness-Based Cognitive Therapy (MBCT) is one such group intervention designed to train recovered, recurrently depressed patients to disengage from thinking and help mediate relapse recurrence. It is based on an integration of cognitive behaviour therapy for depression with mindfulness meditation. Mindfulness meditation, otherwise defined as a receptive attention to, and awareness of, present events and experience (Brown & Ryan, 2003), is one of the major interventions promoted by positive psychology. It is also a practice that has been around for many thousands of years, is a common element of Eastern religions, and is typically associated with Buddhism. It entails the skills of paying attention purposefully, in the present moment and without judgement. MBCT has the goal of reducing relapse and recurrence for those who are vulnerable to episodes of depression and has also been used for other disorders such as stress, anxiety and chronic pain. Based on Jon Kabat-Zinn's practical techniques, MBCT includes simple breathing meditations, body scans and yoga stretches to help participants become more aware of the now, including getting in touch with moment-to-moment changes in the mind and the body. In addition to learning mindfulness meditation techniques, participants are also introduced to simple cognitive-behavioural therapy principles underlying constructive thinking. Supported by several randomized controlled trials, MBCT has emerged as a powerful approach to mood regulation and relapse prevention. A multi-centre randomized control trial was used to allocate 145 recovered participants to either treatment as usual or the same treatment supplemented by MBCT. After receiving eight weeks of classes, participants were followed up for twelve months. The results showed that MBCT was most helpful to those who suffered depression episodes on a number of occasions, reducing the risk of relapse in those who had three or more previous episodes from 66 per cent to 37 per cent (Teasdale et al., 2000).

Tips & Tools
Mindfulness today
Mindfulness can be utilized in many situations, e.g. while cleaning, walking or queuing. It involves effortless concentration and full attentiveness to what you are experiencing or doing at that moment. Simply allow yourself to be absorbed in the here and now, rather than being mentally transported somewhere else. This can enhance your sense of presence (and by doing so your sense of liveliness) and usually has a calming and centring effect.

Positive psychology and business

Well-being at work

Work is enormously important in our lives, not only because it takes up about half of our waking time, or provides us with a means of existence, but also because of the psychological impact that it has. For example, satisfaction with work correlates very well with overall life satisfaction and well-being. Unemployment, on the other hand, is one of the greatest reasons for dissatisfaction with life, depression and negative affect.

Many organizations place a lot of emphasis on the work satisfaction of employees, utilizing research findings to improve working conditions and enhance well-being. Practices and interventions of positive organizations include (Henry, 2004):

- *Job variety.* Enhancing variety and challenge through, for example, cell manufacturing, when groups of workers with different skills see the product from start to finish. This practice can be costly, but it decreases boredom and enhances flow and motivation.
- *Intrinsic motivation.* Although most often, and despite existing knowledge, organizations try to increase their staff's motivation through external rewards such as money (which can kill intrinsic motivation), more attention is being paid nowadays to intrinsic motivation. Some organizations enhance intrinsic motivation through granting their staff free time (e.g. 15 per cent of working time) and even small grants to work on their pet projects (which can sometimes blossom into innovations).
- *Confidence.* Many organizations recognize the dangers of low confidence and negative mindset, and offer training to challenge it. The most extreme forms, such as adventure training and other outdoor challenges, can lead to increased confidence through completing seemingly impossible tasks.
- *Creativity.* Creativity in organizations is enhanced by deliberately recruiting creative individuals and by nurturing creativity in all

staff through problem-solving and other courses (with techniques such as brainstorming, brainwriting, mindmapping and visualization). What is also important is the organizational atmosphere that encourages following hunches and using intuitive understanding, supports innovative ideas, provides resources and facilitates networking.

- *Strengths work* emphasizes building on strengths, rather than focusing only on improving weaknesses. Strengths rhetoric also legitimates a more positive approach to staff development, providing the right environmental conditions for people to flourish (Linley & Harrington, 2005). According to Gallup, many strengths-based developmental interventions have led to a quantifiable impact on *employee engagement* (a commonly used notion in the world of positive organizational psychology) and in turn on performance, productivity, profit and employee turnover. A meta-analysis of over 10,000 work units and 300,000 employees demonstrated that workplaces scoring above the median on the strengths-referenced question 'Do I have the opportunity to do what I do best?' have a 38 per cent greater probability of success in productivity and 44 per cent greater probability of success on customer loyalty and employee retention (Harter & Schmidt, 2002). The strengths approach is also the cornerstone of the process (see below).
- *Team-building* is a common type of intervention, which includes off-site team-building exercises for new teams and personal, interpersonal and group skills training for existing teams.
- *Metaperspective* acknowledges that everything has a positive and negative side. For example, it allows us to see both benefits and downsides of strengths and competences. Metaperspective is a mature approach to personal development, resulting in: balance, acceptance, tolerance and development of the whole person.
- *Flow.* Csikszentmihalyi (2003) believes that our consumer culture devalues work in favour of leisure activities. Even as children we

learn that work is unpleasant, and that everything unpleasant is work. With such attitudes, it is more difficult to achieve flow at work. Moreover, very few jobs nowadays have clear goals (especially goals that are the worker's own), there is rarely adequate feedback beyond 'Are you okay?', skills are infrequently matched with opportunity for action (highly qualified, enthusiastic young professionals often do boring jobs for years), and there is a lack of control at every step of the performance. All the above need to be reversed for flow to occur. Also, the use of time, which usually depends on rhythms not set up by the worker, needs to be made more flexible, open to changing opportunities and internal states of the person.

- *Participatory working practices* come in different forms, including workers having more control over the process of work, working flexible hours, doing telework or a substantial amount from home via email, etc.
- *Open climate, empowerment and self-organization* take participatory working practices to another level. Independence, equality and trust become fundamental in the working process. Employees can challenge established routines, set their own hours, have control over expenses, decide on the share of profits, get rid of bureaucratic departments (e.g. quality control or personnel), hire their own staff, have an open accounting system, and so on. Such practices encourage innovation and flourishing, and result in commitment to the company and high levels of satisfaction and performance.

Positive organizational scholarship

Positive organizational scholarship (POS) is a scientific discipline in its own right that explicitly aims to implement the insights of positive psychology in the workplace. It is generally helpful to consider it as a set of techniques to explore the question of how to help organizations foster well-being as well as meet their commercial or other goals. Thus to a considerable extent it is concerned with describing management techniques that can promote employee well-being, creativity and productivity. The cornerstone of these techniques is promoting a sense of autonomy, self-direction and meaningfulness for workers. On a more personal level, it uses personality assessment techniques developed in positive psychology, such as strengths inventories. POS operates with a number of novel concepts, the most interesting of which are probably positive deviance, high-quality connections and positive leadership.

Positive deviance is defined as intentional behaviour that significantly deviates from the norm in an honourable way, honourable meaning that it improves the human condition in one way or another (Spreitzer & Sonenshein, 2003). Deviance may be a somewhat bizarre word to use, commonly reserved for criminality and implying something bad and forbidden. Arguably, though, 'virtuous' or 'excellent' can also be deviant, in the sense that they deviate from norms. Researchers find that almost every organization contains some individuals whose uncommon but successful behaviours or strategies (often going against HR practices!) enable them to find better solutions to a problem than their peers.

High-quality connections are defined by 'feelings of vitality and aliveness . . . and a heightened sense of positive energy', 'a heightened sense of positive regard' and 'mutuality' (Dutton & Heaphy, 2003). Their benefits include energy and engagement, positive spirals of meaning and organizational strengths. Even a five-minute authentic conversation with a colleague can make a lot of difference. There are five major strategies for encouraging quality connections in the workplace: conveying presence, being genuine, offering affirmation, effective listening and supportive communication.

Finally, *positive leadership* is concerned with enabling effectiveness and exceptional managerial performance through application of research-based principles, such as identification of strengths, fostering virtuousness and facilitation of elevating factors, including optimism, engagement and well-being (author's own definition). Often, positive leadership is what leads to positively deviant performance. As such, it is characterized by four strategies: positive climate, positive relationships, positive communication and positive meaning (Cameron, 2008).

Appreciative inquiry

Appreciative inquiry (AI) is a form of organizational development process that seeks out the best of 'what is' to help ignite the collective imagination of 'what might be', thereby building on strengths to co-create the future (Cooperrider & Whitney, 2005).

The AI process has four stages: discover, dream, design and destiny:

- *Discover*: appreciating the best of what is in the organization.
- *Dream*: creating a shared vision of the future – what could the organization be like at its best? Visual images and metaphor are often used.
- *Design*: what would a strengths-based organization look like and feel like? Making the dream concrete.
- *Destiny*: what will happen to create the future? The group collectively agree who will take what action, playing to individual and team strengths.

AI uses the instrumental pathways of strengths orientation, positive experience and meaning with the aim of generating positive outcomes for individuals and organizations. Speaking more practically, the inquiry induces positive emotions and relatedness, which in turn provides access to 'a world of strengths'. These strengths generate energy that fuels change. There is considerable evidence to support AI as a successful change intervention. The result seems to be a 'movement towards greater equalitarian relationships and self-organising structures' (Cooperrider & Sekerka, 2003).

Even though there is a move towards a more positive orientation, many organizations are still oriented towards fixing the negative (problem-solving, troubleshooting and competences framework) and are clinging on to outdated organizational forms in the fear of losing control over profits. This is where positive psychology, with its empirical backing, can be very useful in evaluating both the subjective and objective impact of the above practices.

Further reading

Biswas-Diener, R. (2010). *Practicing positive psychology coaching*. New York: Wiley.

Boniwell, I., & Ryan, L. (2012). *Personal well-being lessons for secondary schools: Positive psychology in action for 11 to 14 year olds*. Maidenhead: Open University Press.

Cameron, K.S., Dutton, J.E., & Quinn, R.E. (Eds.) (2003). *Positive organizational scholarship*. San Francisco, CA: Berrett-Koehler.

Joseph, S., & Linley, P.A. (2007). *Positive therapy*. New York: Routledge.

Chapter Fifteen
The Future of Positive Psychology

Positive psychology – the state of the field

Today, positive psychology is an active movement with its own national and international conferences, committees, groups and sub-groups, major textbooks and even its own scientific journal. The Positive Psychology Network actively supports the scientific and academic development of young and early-career researchers in its field. I have included, at the end of the book, a list of positive psychology resources for those who might be interested in pursuing their study (or practice) of positive psychology further.

What is right with positive psychology?

When, in 1999, I first heard about positive psychology, I realized immediately that, for me, this was it. It simply made sense. Finally, we had psychology studying interesting topics, rather than something largely irrelevant and unappealing for anyone else but researchers themselves. Finally, it was allowed to use words like 'happiness' and 'character' from the podiums of research conferences and in scientific journals. And finally, distinguished and senior scholars were there to place the soft and fluffy self-help-type topics onto the serious psychological agenda.

Seven years from the moment Martin Seligman (a president of the American Psychological Association at one time) launched positive psychology, the landscape of psychology as a whole had changed. In 1998, the ratio of psychology papers on depression to psychology papers on well-being was 7:1, yet by end of 2005 this ratio was 5:1. In these seven years, nearly five times as many papers were published on hope than on hopelessness, and 3.5 times more articles on optimism than pessimism. Today, psychology is no longer just a science of pathology and depression, operating purely within the disease model, as the science of optimal functioning has firmly established its place under the sun.

What is wrong with positive psychology?

There are a lot of things that are right with positive psychology, yet there are a lot of things that are either wrong or potentially wrong with it. This book has endeavoured to provide a balanced view of this currently flourishing field, illuminating its successes and noting its drawbacks. In this section, I will spend a bit more time concentrating on the latter, highlighting the main critique and problems of positive psychology.

A lack of an acknowledgement of its historical roots

Although positive psychology has a rich history with many predecessors, it is often surprisingly ignorant of previous developments on the topics it studies (many of which are thousands of years old). Not only can this lead to reinventing the wheel yet again, but also to staking claim to someone else's ideas without adequate acknowledgement (Cowen & Kilmer, 2002). Luckily, some positive psychologists agree that acknowledgements are very important, and recognize that better connections with its historical roots would make positive psychology stronger rather than weaker; a little less exotic perhaps, but also less threatening (Peterson & Park, 2003). Attempting to argue that the movement is brand new only leaves an impression of innovation, which disappears if one opens any reference book to an entry of 'happiness'.

A lack of a guiding cohesive theory

At present, an overarching theory of positive psychology, one that can pull together all of the topics that it studies, is lacking. Positive psychology aims to improve too many things, often without knowing exactly what the connections between them are. The very choice of its topics may sometimes be arbitrary. For example, the inclusion of tyranny of freedom seems determined more by chance than by direct relevance (Cowen & Kilmer, 2002).

Reductionist 'scientific' methodology

It is not the first time psychology has attempted to model the study of a person on natural sciences. Many psychologists, although they are prob-ably still in the minority, wonder how such a complex subject as the human being can be studied by a methodology that reduces it to numbers and statistics. Two of the many major problems with adopting such an approach lie in either elaborating the obvious (something that your grandmother knew) or failing to address any important questions. Tennen and Affleck write: 'In its short history, positive psychology has already inherited negative psychology's worst methodological habits' (Tennen & Affleck, 2003).

Drawing big conclusions from weak findings

Even when adopting the mainstream 'scientific' ideology, positive psychology often relies on methods that are cheaper and easier to run. More than half of the studies in the field are so-called *correlation* studies. Correlation studies help to establish that one thing is reliably associated with another (e.g. exercise is associated with better health). However, correlation studies do not allow us to conclude that one thing leads to another – so-called causality. For example, people who exercise might be healthier because of that, or people who are healthier might have more energy to engage in exercise. Even though psychologists know very well that correlations do not imply causality, they often interpret their findings as if they do, leaving an impression that one thing leads to another (Lazarus, 2003a). Beware, marriage is only associated with well-being!

Danger of becoming an ideological movement

'Hooray for positive psychology! Make sure to get on the bandwagon!' These are the types of implicit slogans that prompted several thinkers to assert that positive psychology may be in danger of becoming an ideological movement (Lazarus, 2003b). The many hazards of that include a narrow mindset, resentment of any criticism, hero worship, self-perpetuating beliefs, arrogance and getting stuck in self-imposed positivity, leading to a lack of depth, lack of realism and simplifications.

Positivity as a societal expectation

Professor Barbara Held argues that there is a major 'dark downside' to the positive psychology movement, with a side-effect being that victims of unfortunate circumstances, and other sufferers, are blamed for their own misery. When these people fail to exhibit the necessary optimism, strength, virtue and willpower, this is often interpreted as their own fault. The tyranny of the positive attitude may paradoxically reduce subjective well-being, the very condition it is designed to enhance. The implicit cultural mandate that unhappiness is intolerable and should be abolished may therefore be harmful (Held, 2004). Another Barbara, this time Ehrenreich, found on the discovery of her breast cancer that not only did she have to confront a life-threatening illness but also a whole bunch of pink paraphernalia, from proud cancer-defying slogans on sweatshirts and cuddly teddy bears with a breast-cancer ribbon on their chests through to pink roses in the mammogram changing room. She discovered that as a cancer victim she was almost expected to exude happiness and optimism, and was frowned upon for exposing herself and fellow cancer patients to 'toxic negativity'. This experience became the foundation for her acclaimed book *Smile or Die* (Ehrenreich, 2010), which exposed the pitfalls in positive thinking and positive psychology. Despite being slightly misinterpreted on p. 174 (I really do value sceptical and questioning students!), I find her book a compelling read and tend to agree with the author on several points.

Ignorance of positive aspects of negative thinking

Some research has suggested that mildly depressed older women live longer (Hybels et al., 2002) and that cheerfulness (specifically optimism and sense of humour) was associated with younger age of death in a longitudinal study (Friedman et al., 1993). As discussed in Chapter 3, defensive pessimism can be a good thing, depending on the individual. Furthermore, there is some evidence to support *the case for complaining* (Kowalski, 2002). Although chronic complainers tend to be disliked and the engagement of chronic complaining facilitates negative moods in self and others, there are benefits to such practices. For example, complaining in novel, unpleasant situations can be a good form of social bonding (e.g. when in a waiting room, at a new college or any other unfamiliar situation, expression of complaints about unpleasant circumstances can be an effective ice-breaker).

One-sidedness and lack of balance

Even if you succeeded in engaging in positive thinking and feelings and not paying much attention to the stressful side of life, would that really guarantee you happiness? Or, perhaps, boredom? One of the greatest psychologists of our time, Richard Lazarus, challenges the implicit message of separation between the positive and negative, arguing that these two are just two sides of the same coin: 'Speaking metaphorically rather than mystically, God needs Satan and vice versa. One would not exist without the other. We need the bad, which is part of life, to fully appreciate the good. Any time you narrow the focus of attention too much to one side or another, you are in danger of losing perspective' (Lazarus, 2003a). The realities of life most often fall in between the positive and negative. If the psychology of the past made a major mistake of focusing mainly on the negative, often at the expense of the positive, isn't positive psychology making the same mistake by allowing the pendulum to swing too far to the opposite side? If the proponents of positive psychology are saying that the psychology of the last sixty years is simply incomplete, that is fine, as long as it is not blocked out as a consequence. Positive psychology is in danger of flourishing at the expense of the negative and neutral, rather than contributing to the balanced perspective on a person's life (Lazarus, 2003b). Saying that, some of the contributors to the positive psychology movement appreciate that the dichotomy between the positive and negative may be misleading. Csikszentmihalyi (1992: 69) writes: 'We should reconcile ourselves to the fact that nothing in the world is entirely positive; every power can be misused'.

The words of Tennen and Affleck (2003: 168) serve as a good ending to this rather critical section:

A positive psychology that declares its independence from research in the areas of stress, coping and adaptation; that insists on making qualitative distinctions between seemingly positive and negative human characteristics; that determines a priori and without atten-tion to context those characteristics that will be studied as strengths; that follows psychology's most intractable methodological bad habits and then wears these habits as a merit badge; that distances itself from its predecessors; and dismisses its critics as suspicious and close-minded is, to use Lazarus's terminology, a movement without legs.

If we conceive of psychology as a whole as a dialectic process (Lazarus, 2003a), we can identify 'negative psychology' with the thesis, positive psychology with antithesis, and an integration between these two with synthesis. It is not possible to abandon the opposites (thesis and antithesis), because both are necessary for a synthesis. Some claim that positive psychology is more integrative now, more than twelve years into its existence (Linley & Joseph, 2004b). I wouldn't agree with that. Positive psychology, going through an active period of marketing to the general public, still tries to appear as new and distinct as it can. This is not, however, to say that the integration is not possible.

What does the future hold?

In years to come, it is likely that positive psychology can self-correct at least some of the criticisms discussed above. My hopes for the discipline and its future research areas can be summarized under four 'Cs': context, complexity, creativity and challenge. The *context* point relates to the fact that positive psychology is still largely a Western discipline and little is known about its topics from a cross-cultural perspective. Acknowledging that the research subject of positive psychology is a human being, we cannot avoid the issue of *complexity*. As such, I see the study of unconscious phenomena, social desirability biases, limits of self-awareness and self-knowledge, individual differences (especially when these are greater than inter-group differences) and frequent irrationality of human behaviour as essential for the discipline. When we research factors that enable individuals to thrive, why do we not talk about IQ, or changes that come from realizing you were wrong, or even crying? As it stands, positive psychology is a scientific study of narrowly conceptualized positive phenomena with happiness as a common denominator. To tackle this, we would need some *creativity* in our research designs and also openness to *challenge*.

I do not possess the genius of Alvin Toffler to claim that I can accurately predict the future of positive psychology. It is, however, possible to distinguish between three major potential trajectories. On the one hand, positive psychology may continue as it is at present as a distinct movement, focused on the positive with the help of scientific methods, attracting substantial funding, and (hopefully) delivering substantial findings to the research and general community. On the other hand, in accordance with the predictions of its sceptics, it may turn out to be a fad, a movement without the legs to travel on, failing to discover anything of major significance and falling a victim to its own ideology. On the third hand (if there was such a thing), however, positive psychology may reach the point of synthesis with the so-called 'negative psychology' and its rich heritage, embracing the diversity of available methods, integrating the positive with the negative, and amalgamating all that we know and do not yet know about the most wonderful and fascinating subject matter in the world (the human being) into a coherent whole. In this case, positive psychology will probably cease to exist as an independent movement, yet this is the result I most hope for.

Further reading

Ehrenreich, B. (2009). *Smile or die: How positive thinking fooled America and the world*. London: Granta Books.
Held, B.S. (2001). *Stop smiling, start kvetching: A 5-step guide to creative complaining*. New York: St Martin's Griffin.

Internet Resources

http://www.positivepsychology.org
The main positive psychology website provides a comprehensive overview of current activities and offers a VIA strengths inventory for
completion and immediate feedback.

http://www.ippanetwork.org/
The website of the International Positive Psychology Association
(IPPA), whose mission is to promote the science and practice of positive psychology and to facilitate communication and collaboration
among researchers and practitioners around the world.

http://enpp.org
The European Network of Positive Psychology website offers information on positive psychology activities in Europe.

http://www.positivepsychology.org.uk
The first go-to positive psychology website in the UK, offering articles,
questionnaires, information about educational opportunities and updates
on current events.

http://www1.eur.nl/fsw/happiness/index.html
This website provides an ongoing register of scientific research on subjective appreciation of life hosted by one of the leading researchers.

http://www.authentichappiness.org
The Authentic Happiness website allows you to access many positive psychology tests and questionnaires. Although it is completely free, you are required to register.

http://www.actionforhappiness.org/
Action for Happiness is a UK movement for positive social change.

http://pos-psych.com/
Positive Psychology News Daily brings a daily dose of positive psychology into your inbox.

http://www.strengthsquest.com
Use this Gallup website to discover your work-related strengths. The web-based questionnaire is not free, but affordable.

http://www.uel.ac.uk/psychology/programmes/postgraduate/positive-msc.htm
Here you will find useful information about the MSc in Applied Positive Psychology at the University of East London.

http://psych.rochester.edu/SDT/index.html
This self-determination theory website is a good resource for those who would like to find out more about this field of research.

http://www.centreforconfidence.co.uk/
This Glasgow-based centre disseminates learning from positive psychology. See their excellent resources section for a comprehensive overview of many positive psychology topics.

http://www.bus.umich.edu/Positive/
The Centre for Positive Organizational Scholarship website offers many resources to those who are interested in applying positive psychology to organizations.

http://www.cambridgewellbeing.org/
The Well-being Institute is a cross-disciplinary initiative that aims to promote the highest quality research in the science of well-being, and to integrate this research into first-rate evidence-based practice.

http://www.cappeu.org/
The Centre for Applied Positive Psychology is a private consultancy that focuses on the applications of strengths research and houses questionnaires for Realise2.

http://www.neweconomics.org/gen/hottopics_well-being.aspx
The New Economics Foundation's well-being programme aims to promote policies that help people live more fulfilled lives.

http://www.positran.co.uk
Psychology for Positive Transformation, or Positran, in short, is a private website of Dr Boniwell, which lists her consultancy activities and speaking engagements.

References

Allport, G.W. (1955). *Becoming.* New Haven, CT: Yale University Press.

Argyle, M. (2001). *The psychology of happiness.* Hove, UK: Routledge.

Aron, E.N., & Aron, A. (1996). Love and expansion of the self: The state of the model. *Personal Relationships, 3,* 45–58.

Babyak, M., Blumenthal, J.A., Herman, S., Khatri, P., Doraiswamy, M., Moore, K. et al. (2000). Exercise treatment for major depression: Maintenance of therapeutic benefit at 10 months. *Psychosomatic Medicine, 62,* 633–638.

Bachkirova, T., & Coz, E. (2004). A bridge over troubled water: Bringing together coaching and counselling. *International Journal of Mentoring and Coaching, 2*(1).

Baltes, P.B. (1987). Theoretical propositions of life-span developmental psychology: On the dynamics between growth and decline. *Developmental Psychology, 23,* 611–626.

Baltes, P.B., & Freund, A.M. (2003). Human strengths as the orchestration of wisdom and selective optimization with compensation. In L.G. Aspinwall & U.M. Staudinger (Eds.), *A psychology of human strengths* (pp. 23–35). Washington, DC: American Psychological Association.

Baltes, P.B., Staudinger, U.M., Maercker, A., & Smith, J. (1995). People nominated as wise: A comparative study of wisdom-related knowledge. *Psychology and Aging, 10,* 155–166.

Bandura, A. (1997). *Self-efficacy.* New York: Freeman.

Banks, R. (1983). *The tyranny of time.* Downers Grove, IL: InterVarsity Press.

Baumeister, R.F., & Vohs, K.D. (2002). The pursuit of meaningfulness in life. In C.R. Snyder & S.J. Lopez (Eds.), *Handbook of positive psychology* (pp. 608–618). New York: Oxford University Press.

173

Belsky, J., & Pluess, M. (2008). The nature (and nurture?) of plasticity in early human development. *Perspectives in Psychological Science, 4*, 345–351.

Ben-Shahar, T. (2007). *Happier*. New York: McGraw-Hill.

Berscheid, E. (2003). The human's greatest strength: Other humans. In L.G. Aspinwall & U.M. Staudinger (Eds.), *A psychology of human strengths* (pp. 37–48). Washington, DC: American Psychological Association.

Boehnke, K., Schwartz, S.H., Stromberg, C., & Sagiv, L. (1998). The structure and dynamics of worry: Theory, measurement, and cross-cultural replications. *Journal of Personality, 66*, 745–782.

Boniwell, I. (2009). *Time for life: Satisfaction with time use and its relationship with subjective well-being*. Saarbrücken: VDM.

Boniwell, I., & Osin, E. (in prep.). Development and validation of a eudaimonic well-being scale.

Boniwell, I., & Ryan, L. (2012). *Personal well-being lessons for secondary schools: Positive psychology in action for 11 to 14 year olds*. Maidenhead: Open University Press.

Boniwell, I., & Zimbardo, P.G. (2003). Time to find the right balance. *The Psychologist, 16*, 129–131.

Boniwell, I., & Zimbardo, P.G. (2004). Balancing time perspective in pursuit of optimal functioning. In P.A. Linley & S. Joseph (Eds.), *Positive psychology in practice* (pp. 165–178). Hoboken, NJ: Wiley.

Boniwell, I., Osin, E., Linley, P.A., & Ivanchenko, G. (2010). A question of balance: Examining relationships between time perspective and measures of well-being in the British and Russian student samples. *Journal of Positive Psychology, 5*, 24–40.

Boniwell, I., Pluess, M., Hefferon, K., & Tunariu., A. (in prep.). Validation of SPARK Resilience Curriculum for Y7 and Y8 students.

Brickman, P., Coates, D., & Janoff-Bulman, R. (1978). Lottery winners and accident victims: Is happiness relative? *Journal of Personality and Social Psychology, 36*, 917–927.

Brown, K., & Ryan, R. (2003). The benefits of being present: Mindfulness and its role in psychological well-being. *Journal of Personality and Social Psychology, 84*, 822–848.

Brown, K.W., & Ryan, R.M. (2004). Fostering healthy self-regulation from within and without: A self-determination theory perspective. In P.A. Linley and S. Joseph (Eds.), *Positive psychology in practice* (pp. 105–124). Hoboken, NJ: Wiley.

Brunwasser, S.M., Gillham, J.E., & Kim, E.S. (2009). A meta-analytic review of the Penn Resiliency Program's effect on depressive symptoms. *Journal of Consulting and Clinical Psychology, 77,* 1042–1054.

Bryant, F.B., & Veroff, J. (2007). *Savouring: A new model of positive experiences.* Mahwah, NJ: Lawrence Erlbaum Associates.

Bryant, F.B., Smart, C.M., & King, S.P. (2005). Using the past to enhance the presence: Boosting happiness through positive reminiscence. *Journal of Happiness Studies, 6,* 227–260.

Cameron, K. (2008). *Positive leadership: Strategies for extraordinary performance.* San Francisco, CA: Berrett-Koehler.

Campos, J.J. (2003). When the negative becomes positive and the reverse: Comments on Lazarus's critique of positive psychology. *Psychological Inquiry, 14,* 110–113.

Carr, A. (2004). *Positive psychology.* Hove, UK: Brunner-Routledge.

Carroll, M. (2003). The new kid on the block. *Counselling Psychology Journal, 14*(10), 28–31.

Carstensen, L.L., & Charles, S.T. (2003). Human aging: Why is even good news taken as bad? In L.G. Aspinwall & U.M. Staudinger (Eds.), *A psychology of human strengths* (pp. 75–86). Washington, DC: American Psychological Association.

Carstensen, L.L., Gottman, J.M., & Levenson, R.W. (1995). Emotional behaviour in long-term marriage. *Psychology and Aging, 10,* 140–149.

Carver, C.S., & Scheier, M.F. (2002). Optimism. In C.R. Snyder & S.J. Lopez (Eds.), *Handbook of positive psychology.* New York: Oxford University Press.

Casey, B.J., Somerville, L.H., Gotlib, I., Ayduk, O., Franklin, N., Askren, M.K. et al. (2011). Behavioral and neural correlates of delay of gratification 40 years later. *Proceedings of the National Academy of Sciences USA, 108,* 14998–15003.

Christakis, N., & Fowler, J. (2009). *Connected: The surprising power of our social networks and how they shape our lives.* New York: Little, Brown.

Ciarrocchi, J.W., Dy-Liacco, G., & Deneke, E. (2008). Gods or rituals? Relational faith, spiritual discontent, and religious practices as predictors of hope and optimism. *Journal of Positive Psychology, 3,* 120–136.

Clifton, D.O., & Anderson, E.C. (2001–02). *StrengthsQuest*. Washington, DC: Gallup Organization.

Clow, A., & Fredhoi, C. (2006). Normalisation of salivary cortisol levels and self-report stress by a brief lunchtime visit to an art gallery by London City workers. *Journal of Holistic Healthcare, 3*(2), 29–32.

Cohen, S., Doyle, W.J., Turner, R.B., Alper, C.M., & Skoner, D.P. (2003). Sociability and susceptibility to the common cold. *Psychological Science, 14*, 389–395.

Compte-Sponville, A. (2004). *The little book of philosophy*. London: William Heinemann.

Compton, W.C., Smith, M.L., Cornish, K.A., & Qualls, D.L. (1996). Factor structure of mental health measures. *Journal of Personality and Social Psychology, 71*, 406–413.

Cooperrider, D.L., & Sekerka, L.E. (2003). Towards a theory of positive organisational change. In K.S. Cameron, J.E. Dutton, & R.E. Quinn (Eds.), *Positive organizational scholarship: Foundations of a new discipline* (pp. 225–240). San Francisco, CA: Berrett-Koehler.

Cooperrider, D.L., & Whitney, D. (2005). *Appreciative inquiry: A positive revolution in change*. San Francisco, CA: Berrett-Koehler.

Cowen, E.I. (1994). The enhancement of psychological wellness: Challenges and opportunities. *American Journal of Community Psychology, 22*, 149–179.

Cowen, E.L., & Kilmer, R.P. (2002). 'Positive psychology': Some pluses and some open issues. *Journal of Community Psychology, 30*, 449–460.

Cowen, E.I., Gardner, E.A., & Zax, M. (Eds.) (1967). *Emergent approaches to mental health problems: An overview and directions for future work*. New York: Appleton-Century-Crofts.

Csikszentmihalyi, M. (1992). *Flow: The psychology of happiness*. London: Rider.

Csikszentmihalyi, M. (1997). *Finding flow*. New York: Basic Books.

Csikszentmihalyi, M. (2003). *Good business*. London: Hodder & Stoughton.

Danish, S.J. (1996). Going for the goal: A life-skills program for adolescents. In G.W. Abele & T.P. Gullotta (Eds.), *Primary prevention works* (pp. 291–312). Thousand Oaks, CA: Sage.

Danner, D., Snowdon, D., & Friesen, W. (2001). Positive emotion early in life and longevity: Findings from the nun study. *Journal of Personality and Social Psychology, 80*, 804–813.

De Botton, A. (2005). *Status anxiety*. London: Penguin Books.

Delle Fave, A., & Massimini, F. (2004a). Bringing subjectivity into focus: Optimal experiences, life themes, and person-centred rehabilitation. In P.A. Linley and S. Joseph (Eds.), *Positive psychology in practice* (pp. 581–597). Hoboken, NJ: Wiley.

Delle Fave, A., & Massimini, F. (2004b). The cross-cultural investigation of optimal experience. *Ricerche di Psicologia, 27*, 79–102.

De Shazer, S., Dolan, Y., & Korman, H. (2007). *More than miracles: The state of the art of solution-focused brief therapy*. New York: Haworth Press.

Diener, E. (1984). Subjective well-being. *Psychological Bulletin, 95*, 542–575.

Diener, E. (1999). Subjective well-being: Three decades of progress. *Psychological Bulletin, 125*, 276–301.

Diener, E. (2000). Subjective well-being: The science of happiness and a proposal for a national index. *American Psychologist, 55*, 56–67.

Diener, E. (2001). The benefits of positive affect and happiness. Paper presented at the Positive Psychology Summer Institute 2001, Sea Ranch, CA.

Diener, E. (2003). What is positive about positive psychology: The Curmudgeon and Pollyanna. *Psychological Inquiry, 14*, 115–120.

Diener, E., & Fujita, F. (1995). Resources, personal strivings, and subjective well-being: A nomothetic and idiographic approach. *Journal of Personality and Social Psychology, 68*, 926–935.

Diener, E., & Seligman, M.E.P. (2002). Very happy people. *Psychological Science, 13*, 81–84.

Diener, E., Emmons, R.A., Larson, R.J., & Griffin, S. (1985). The Satisfaction With Life Scale. *Journal of Personality Assessment, 49*, 71–75.

Diener, E., Sandvik, E., & Pavot, W. (1991). Happiness is the frequency, not the intensity, of positive versus negative affect. In F. Strack, M. Argyle, & N. Schwarz (Eds.), *Subjective well-being: An interdisciplinary perspective* (pp. 119–139). Elmsford, NY: Pergamon Press.

Diener, E., Diener, M., & Diener, C. (1995). Factors predicting the subjective well-being of nations. *Journal of Personality and Social Psychology, 69*, 851–864.

Diener, E., Lucas, E.L., & Oishi, S. (2001). Subjective well-being. In C.R. Snyder & S.J. Lopez (Eds.), *Handbook of positive psychology* (pp. 63–73). New York: Oxford University Press.

Drake, L., Duncan, E., Sutherland, F., Abernethy, C., & Henry, C. (2008). Time perspective and correlates of wellbeing. *Time and Society, 17*(1), 47–61.

Duckworth, A.L., Peterson, C., Matthews, M.D., & Kelly, D.R. (2007). Grit: Perseverance and passion for long-term goals. *Personality Processes and Individual Differences, 92,* 1087–1101.

Dunn, E.W., Aknin, L.B., & Norton, M.I. (2008). Spending money on others promotes happiness. *Science, 319,* 1687–1688.

Dutton, J.E., & Heaphy, E.D. (2003). The power of high-quality connections. In K.S. Cameron, J.E. Dutton, & R.E. Quinn (Eds.), *Positive organizational scholarship: Foundations of a new discipline* (pp. 263–279). San Francisco, CA: Berrett-Koehler.

Dweck, C. (2006). *Mindset: The new psychology of success.* New York: Random House.

Easterlin, R.A., Angelescu McVey, L., Switek, M., Swangfa, O., & Zweig Smith, J. (2010). The happiness–income paradox revisited. *Proceedings of the National Academy of Sciences USA, 107,* 22463–22468.

Ehrenreich, B. (2010). *Smile or die: How positive thinking fooled America and the world.* New York: Granta Books.

Emmons, R. (2007). *Thanks! How the new science of gratitude can make you happier.* New York: Houghton Mifflin.

Farina, C.J., Hearth, A.K., & Popovich, J.M. (1995). *Hope and hopelessness: Critical clinical constructs.* Thousand Oaks, CA: Sage.

Fava, G., & Ruini, C. (2009). Well-being therapy. In S. Lopez (Ed), *The encyclopedia of positive psychology* (pp. 1034–1036). Chichester: Blackwell Publishing.

Ford, M.E., & Nichols, C.W. (1991). Using goals assessment to identify motivational patterns and facilitate behavioural regulation and achievement. *Advances in Motivation and Achievement, 7,* 51–84.

Frankl, V.E. (1963). *Man's search for meaning: An introduction to logotherapy.* New York: Washington Square Press.

Fredrickson, B.L. (2001). The role of positive emotions in positive psychology: The broaden-and-build theory of positive emotions. *American Psychologist, 56,* 218–226.

Fredrickson, B.L. (2002). Positive emotions. In C.R. Snyder & S.J. Lopez (Eds.), *Handbook of positive psychology* (pp. 120–134). New York: Oxford University Press.

Fredrickson, B.L. (2004). The broaden-and-build theory of positive emotions. *Philosophical Transactions of the Royal Society of London B, 359*, 1367–1378.

Fredrickson, B. (2009) *Positivity*. New York: Crown.

Freese, J., Meland, S., & Irwin, W. (2006). Expressions of positive emotion in photographs, personality, and later-life marital and health outcomes. *Journal of Research in Personality, 41*, 488–497.

Friedman, H.S., Tucker, J.S., Tomlinson-Keasey, C., Schwartz, J.E, Wingard, D.L., & Criqui, M.H. (1993). Does childhood personality predict longevity? *Journal of Personality and Social Psychology, 65*, 176–185.

Frisch, M.B. (2006). *Quality of life therapy: Applying a life satisfaction approach to positive psychology and cognitive therapy*. Hoboken, NJ: Wiley.

Froh, J.J., Fives, C.J., Fuller, J.R., Jacofsky, M.D., Terjesen, M.D., & Yurkewicz, C. (2007). Interpersonal relationships and irrationality as predictors of life satisfaction. *Journal of Positive Psychology, 2*, 29–39.

Fromm, E. (1957/1995). *The art of loving*. London: Thorsons.

Fromm, E. (1976). *To have or to be?* New York: Continuum.

Gable, S.L., Reis, H.T., Asher, E.R., & Impett, E.A. (2004). What do you do when things go right? The intrapersonal and interpersonal benefits of sharing positive events. *Journal of Personality and Social Psychology, 87*, 228–245.

Gottman, J. (1993). The roles of conflict engagement, escalation and avoidance in marital interaction: A longitudinal view of five types of couples. *Journal of Consulting and Clinical Psychology, 61*, 6–15.

Gottman, J., & Levenson, R.W. (2002). A two-factor model for predicting when a couple will divorce: Exploratory analyses using 14-year longitudinal data. *Family Process, 41*, 83–96.

Harker, L., & Keltner, D. (2001). Expressions of positive emotion in women's college yearbook pictures and their relationship to personality and life outcomes across adulthood. *Journal of Personality and Social Psychology, 80*, 112–124.

Harter, J.K., & Schmidt, F.L. (2002). *Employee engagement, satisfaction and business-unit level outcomes: Meta-analysis*. Princeton, NJ: Gallup Organization.

Hartfield, E. (1988). Passionate and compassionate love. In R.J. Sternberg & M.L. Barnes (Eds.), *The psychology of love* (pp. 191–217). New Haven, CT: Yale University Press.

Harvey, J.H., Pauwels, B.G., & Zickmund, S. (2004). Relationship connection. In C.R. Snyder & S.J. Lopez (Eds.), *Handbook of positive psychology* (pp. 423–433). New York: Oxford University Press.

Hayes, S.C., Strosahl, K.D., & Wilson, K.G. (1999). *Acceptance and commitment therapy: An experiential approach to behavior change.* New York: Guilford Press.

Hefferon, K., & Boniwell, I. (2011). *Positive psychology: Theory, research and applications.* Oxford: Open University Press.

Held, B.S. (2004). The negative side of positive psychology. *Journal of Humanistic Psychology, 44*, 9–46.

Hendrick, S., & Hendrick, C. (2002). Love. In C.R. Snyder & S.J. Lopez (Eds.), *Handbook of positive psychology* (pp. 472–484). New York: Oxford University Press.

Henry, J. (2004). Positive and creative organisations. In P.A. Linley and S. Joseph (Eds.), *Positive psychology in practice* (pp. 269–287). Hoboken, NJ: Wiley.

Hertenstein, M.J., Hansel, C., Butts, A.M., & Hile, S. (2009). Smile intensity in photographs predicts divorce later in life. *Motivation and Emotion, 33*, 99–105.

Hodges, T.D., & Clifton, D.O. (2004). Strength-based development in practice. In P.A. Linley & S. Joseph (Eds.), *Positive psychology in practice* (pp. 256–268). Hoboken, NJ: Wiley.

Huta, V. (in press). The difference between eudaimonia and hedonia. In S. David, I. Boniwell, & A. Conley (Eds.), *Oxford handbook of happiness.* Oxford: Oxford University Press.

Huta, V., Park, N., Peterson, C., & Seligman, M.E.P. (2003). Pursuing pleasure versus eudaimonia: Which leads to greater satisfaction? Poster presented at the 2nd International Positive Psychology Summit, Washington, DC.

Hybels, C., Pieper, C., & Blazer, D. (2002). Sex differences in the relationship between subthreshold depression and mortality in a community sample of older adults. *American Journal of Geriatric Psychiatry, 10*, 283–291.

Isen, A.M. (2002). Positive affect as a source of human strength. In L.G. Aspinwall & U.M. Staudinger (Eds.), *A psychology of human strengths.* Washington, DC: American Psychological Association.

Isen, A.M., Rozentzweig, A.S., & Young, M.J. (1991). The influence of positive affect on clinical problem solving. *Medical Decision Making, 11*, 221–227.

Jahoda, M. (1958). *Current concepts of positive mental health.* New York: Basic Books.

Joseph, S., & Linley, P.A. (2005). Positive adjustment to threatening events: An organismic valuing theory of growth through adversity. *Review of General Psychology, 9*, 262–280.

Joseph, S., & Linley, P.A. (2007). *Positive therapy.* New York: Routledge.

Jung, C.G. (1933). *Modern man in search of a soul.* New York: Harcourt, Brace & World.

Jyengar, S., & Lepper, M. (2000). When choice is demotivating: Can one desire too much of a good thing? *Journal of Personality and Social Psychology, 79*, 995–1006.

Kahana, E., & Kahana, B. (1983). Environmental continuity, futurity and adaptation of the aged. In G.D. Rowles & R.J. Ohta (Eds.), *Aging and milieu* (pp. 205–228). New York: Haworth Press.

Kahneman, D. (1999). Objective happiness. In D. Kahneman, E. Diener, & N. Schwarz (Eds.), *Well-being: The foundations of hedonic psychology* (pp. 3–25). New York: Russell Sage.

Kashdan, T.B., Biswas-Diener, R., & King, L.A. (2008). Reconsidering happiness: The costs of distinguishing between hedonics and eudaimonia. *Journal of Positive Psychology, 3*, 219–233.

Kasser, T. (2002). *The high price of materialism.* Cambridge, MA: MIT Press.

Kasser, T., & Ryan, R.M. (1996). Further examining the American dream: Differential correlates of intrinsic and extrinsic goals. *Personality and Social Psychology Bulletin, 22*, 280–287.

Kasser, T., & Sheldon, K.M. (2009). Time affluence as a path towards personal happiness and ethical business practices: Empirical evidence from four studies. *Journal of Business Ethics, 84*, 243–255.

Kauffman, C., & Scoular, A. (2004). Towards a positive psychology of executive coaching. In P.A. Linley and S. Joseph (Eds.), *Positive psychology in practice* (pp. 287–302). Hoboken, NJ: Wiley.

Kauffman, C., Boniwell, I., & Silberman, J. (2009). Positive psychology coaching. In T. Bachkirova, E. Duncan, & D. Clutterbuck (Eds.), *The Sage handbook of coaching* (pp. 158–171). London: Sage.

Kazakina, E. (1999). Time perspective of older adults: Relationships to attachment style, psychological well-being and psychological distress. Unpublished doctoral dissertation, Columbia University.

Keltner, D., & Bonanno, G.A. (1997). A study of laughter and dissociation: The distinct correlates of laughter and smiling during bereavement. *Journal of Personality and Social Psychology, 73,* 687–702.

Keyes, C.L.M., Shmotkin, D., & Ryff, C.D. (2002). Optimizing well-being: the empirical encounter of two traditions. *Journal of Personality and Social Psychology, 82,* 1007–1022.

King, L.A., & Napa, C.K. (1998). What makes a life good? *Journal of Personality and Social Psychology, 75,* 156–165.

Kobrin, F.E., & Hendershot, G.E. (1977). Do family ties reduce mortality? Evidence from the United States 1966–1968. *Journal of Marriage and the Family, 39,* 737–745.

Kowalski, R. (2002). Whining, griping, and complaining: Positivity in the negativity. *Journal of Clinical Psychology, 58,* 1023–1035.

Kunzmann, U. (2004). Approaches to a good life: The emotional-motivational side to wisdom. In P.A. Linley & S. Joseph (Eds.), *Positive psychology in practice* (pp. 504–517). Hoboken, NJ: Wiley.

Lambert, M., & Barley, D. (2002). Research summary on the therapeutic relationship and psychotherapy outcome. In J. Norcross (Ed.), *Psychotherapy relationships that work.* New York: Basic Books.

Lane, R.E. (1995). Time preferences: The economics of work and leisure. *Demos, 5,* 35–44.

Lazarus, R.S. (2003a). Does the positive psychology movement have legs? *Psychological Inquiry, 14,* 93–109.

Lazarus, R.S. (2003b). The Lazarus manifesto for positive psychology and psychology in general. *Psychological Inquiry, 14,* 173–189.

Linley, A. (2011). *The Realise 2 4M model.* Accessed at: http://www.cappeu.com/Realise2/TheRealise24MModel.aspx

Linley, A., Willars, J., & Biswas-Diener, R. (2010). *The strengths book.* Coventry: CAPP Press.

Linley, P.A. & Harrington, S. (2005). Positive psychology and coaching psychology: perspectives on integration. *The Coaching Psychologist, 1*(1), 13–14.

Linley, P.A., & Harrington, S. (2006). Playing to your strengths. *The Psychologist*, 19, 86–89.

Linley, P.A., & Joseph, S. (2004a). Positive changes following trauma and adversity: A review. *Journal of Traumatic Stress Studies*, 17, 11–21.

Linley, P.A., & Joseph, S. (2004b). Towards a theoretical foundation for positive psychology in practice. In P.A. Linley & S. Joseph (Eds.), *Positive psychology in practice* (pp. 713–731). Hoboken, NJ: Wiley.

Locke, E.A. (2002). Setting goals for life and happiness. In C.R. Snyder & S.J. Lopez (Eds.), *Handbook of positive psychology* (pp. 299–313). New York: Oxford University Press.

Lopez, S.J., Snyder, C.R., Magyar-Moe, J.L., Edwards, L.M., Pedrotti, J.T., Janowksi, K. et al. (2004). Strategies for accentuating hope. In P.A. Linley and S. Joseph (Eds.), *Positive psychology in practice* (pp. 388–403). Hoboken, NJ: Wiley.

Lupien, S.J., & Wan, N. (2004). Successful ageing: From cell to cell. *Philosophical Transactions of the Royal Society of London B*, 359, 1413–1426.

Lyubomirsky, S. (2001). Why are some people happier than others? The role of cognitive and motivational processes in well-being. *American Psychologist*, 56, 239–249.

Lyubomirsky, S. (2008). *The HOW of happiness*. London: Sphere.

Macan, T.H. (1994). Time management: Test of a process model. *Journal of Applied Psychology*, 79, 381–391.

Macan, T.H. (1996). Time-management training: Effects on time behaviours, attitudes, and job performance. *Journal of Psychology*, 130, 229–237.

Macan, T.H., Shahani, C., Dipboye, R.L., & Phillips, A.P. (1990). College students' time management: Correlations with academic performance and stress. *Journal of Educational Psychology*, 82, 760–768.

Maslow, A. (1968). *Towards a psychology of being*. New York: Van Nostrand Reinhold.

Mayer, J., DiPaola, M., & Salovey, P. (1990). Perceiving affective content in ambiguous visual stimuli: A component of emotional intelligence. *Journal of Personality Assessment*, 54, 772–781.

McGrath, H., & Noble, T. (2003). *Bounce back! Teacher's handbook*. Sydney, NSW: Pearson Education.

McGregor, I., & Little, B.R. (1998). Personal projects, happiness, and meaning: On doing well and being yourself. *Journal of Personality and Social Psychology*, 74, 494–512.

Morris, I. (2009). *Teaching happiness and well-being in schools: Learning to ride elephants*. London: Continuum International Publishing.

Myers, D.G. (2000). The funds, friends, and faith of happy people. *American Psychologist*, 55, 56–67.

Myers, D.M. (1992). *The pursuit of happiness*. New York: Morrow.

Newman, B., & Newman, P. (1991). *Development through life* (5th edn.). Pacific Grove, CA: Brooks/Cole.

Nolen-Hoeksema, S., & Davis, C.G. (2002). Positive responses to loss. In C.R. Snyder & S.J. Lopez (Eds.), *Handbook of positive psychology* (pp. 598–607). New York: Oxford University Press.

Norem, J.K., & Chang, E.C. (2002). The positive psychology of negative thinking. *Journal of Clinical Psychology*, 58, 993–1001.

Oatley, K., & Jenkins, J. (1996). *Understanding emotions*. Oxford: Blackwell.

Oishi, S., Diener, E., Suh, E., & Lucas, R.E. (1999). Value as a moderator in subjective well-being. *Journal of Personality*, 67, 157–184.

Palmer, S., & Whybrow, A. (2005). The proposal to establish a special group in coaching psychology. *The Coaching Psychologist*, 1, 5–12.

Peltier, B. (2001). *The psychology of executive coaching*. Hove: Brunner-Routledge.

Pentland, W.E., Harvey, A.S., Lawton, M.P., & McColl, M.A. (Eds.) (1999). *Time use research in the social sciences*. New York: Kluwer Academic/Plenum Publishers.

Person, C., Seligman, M.E.P., & Vaillant, G.E. (1988). Pessimistic explanatory style is a risk factor for physical illness: A thirty-five years longitudinal study. *Journal of Personality and Social Psychology*, 55, 23–27.

Peterson, C., & Park, N. (2003). Positive psychology as the even-handed positive psychologist views it. *Psychological Inquiry*, 14, 143–147.

Peterson, C., & Seligman, M.E.P. (2004). *Character strengths and virtues: A handbook and classification*. Washington, DC: American Psychological Association.

Popovic, N. (2002). An outline of a new model of personal education. *Pastoral Care*, 20, 12–20.

Popovic, N. (2005). *Personal synthesis*. London: PWBC.

Popovic, N., & Boniwell, I. (2007). Personal consultancy: An integrative approach to one-to-one talking practices. *International Journal of Evidence Based Coaching and Mentoring*, 5 (special issue), 24–29.

Privette, G. (1983). Peak experience, peak performance, and peak flow: A comparative analysis of positive human experiences. *Journal of Personality and Social Psychology*, 45, 1369–1379.

Rath, T., & Harter, J. (2010). *Wellbeing: The five essential elements*. New York: Gallup Press.

Reivich, K.J., Gillham, J.E., Chaplin, T.M., & Seligman, M.E.P. (2005). From helplessness to optimism: The role of resilience in treating and preventing depression in youth. In S. Goldstein & R.B. Brooks (Eds.), *Handbook of resilience in children* (pp. 223–237). New York: Kluwer Academic/Plenum Publishers.

Reznitskaya, A., & Sternberg, R.J. (2004). Teaching students to make wise judgements: The 'Teaching for Wisdom' programme. In P.A. Linley & S. Joseph (Eds.), *Positive psychology in practice* (pp. 181–196). Hoboken, NJ: Wiley.

Robbins, A.S., Spence, J.T., & Clark, H. (1991). Psychological determinants of health and performance: The tangled web of desirable and undesirable characteristics. *Journal of Personality and Social Psychology*, 61, 755–765.

Robinson, J.P., & Godbey, G. (1997). *Time for life: The surprising ways Americans use their time*. State College, PA: The Pennsylvania State University Press.

Rogers, C.R. (1961). *On becoming a person: The struggle toward self-realization*. London: Constable.

Ryan, R.M., & Deci, E.L. (2000). Self-determination theory and the facilitation of intrinsic motivation, social development and well-being. *American Psychologist*, 55, 68–78.

Ryan, R.M., & Deci, E.L. (2001). On happiness and human potentials: A review of research on hedonic and eudaimonic well-being. *Annual Review of Psychology*, 52, 141–166.

Ryff, C.D., & Keyes, C.L.M. (1995). The structure of psychological well-being revisited. *Journal of Personality and Social Psychology*, 69, 719–727.

Ryff, C.D., & Singer, B. (1998). The contours of positive human health. *Psychological Inquiry*, 9, 1–28.

Ryff, C.D., Singer, B.H., & Love, G.D. (2004). Positive health: Connecting well-being with biology. *Philosophical Transactions of the Royal Society of London B*, 359, 1383–1394.

Salovey, P., & Mayer, J. (1990). Emotional intelligence. *Imagination, Cognition and Personality*, 9, 185–211.

Salovey, P., Mayer, J.D., & Caruso, D. (2002). The positive psychology of emotional intelligence. In C.R. Snyder & S.J. Lopez (Eds.), *Handbook of positive psychology* (pp. 159–171). New York: Oxford University Press.

Salovey, P., Caruso, D., & Mayer, J.D. (2004). Emotional intelligence in practice. In P.A. Linley and S. Joseph (Eds.), *Positive psychology in practice* (pp. 447–463). Hoboken, NJ: Wiley.

Schwartz, B. (2000). Self-determination: The tyranny of freedom. *American Psychologist*, 55, 79–88.

Schwartz, B. (2004). *A paradox of choice: Why more can be less.* New York: HarperCollins.

Schwartz, B., & Ward, A. (2004). Doing better but feeling worse: The paradox of choice. In P.A. Linley and S. Joseph (Eds.), *Positive psychology in practice* (pp. 86–104). Hoboken, NJ: Wiley.

Schmuck, P., & Sheldon, K.M. (2001.) *Life goals and well-being: Towards a positive psychology of human striving.* Kirkland, WA: Hogrefe & Huber.

Schneider, S. (2001). In search of realistic optimism: Meaning, knowledge, and warm fuzziness. *American Psychologist*, 56, 250–263.

Schwartz, S.H. (1994). Are there universal aspects in the content and structure of values? *Journal of Social Issues*, 50, 19–46.

Schwartz, S.H., Sagiv, L., & Boehnke, K. (2000). Worries and values. *Journal of Personality*, 68, 309–346.

Seligman, M.E.P. (1991). *Learned optimism.* New York: Knopf.

Seligman, M.E.P. (2002). *Authentic happiness.* New York: Free Press.

Seligman, M.E.P. (2011). *Flourish: A new understanding of happiness and well-being and how to achieve them.* London: Nicholas Brealey.

Seligman, M.E.P., & Csikszentmihalyi, M. (2000). Positive psychology: An introduction. *American Psychologist*, 55, 5–14.

Seligman, M.E.P., & Peterson, C. (2003). Positive clinical psychology. In L.G. Aspinwall & U.M. Staudinger (Eds.), *A psychology of human strengths* (pp. 305–317). Washington, DC: American Psychological Association.

Seligman, M.E.P., & Schulman, P. (1986). Explanatory style as a predictor of productivity and quitting among life insurance agents. *Journal of Personality and Social Psychology*, 50, 832–838.

Seligman, M.E.P., Steen, T., Park, N., Peterson, P. (2005). Positive psychology progress: Empirical validation of interventions. *American Psychologist*, 60, 410–421.

Sheldon, K.M. (1994). The Self-Concordance Model of healthy goal striving: When personal goals correctly represent the person. In P. Schmuck & K.M. Sheldon (Eds.), *Life goals and well-being: Towards a positive psychology of human striving*. Kirkland, WA: Hogrefe & Huber.

Sheldon, K.M., & Lyubomirsky, S. (2004). Achieving sustainable new happiness: Prospects, practices and prescriptions. In P.A. Linley & S. Joseph (Eds.), *Positive psychology in practice* (pp. 127–145). Hoboken, NJ: Wiley.

Shoda, Y., Mischel, W., & Peake, P.K. (1990). Predicting adolescent cognitive and self-regulatory competencies from preschool delay of gratification: Identifying diagnostic conditions. *Developmental Psychology*, 26, 978–986.

Snyder, C.R., Rand, K.L., & Sigmon, D.R. (2002). Hope theory: A member of the positive psychology family. In C.R. Snyder & S.J. Lopez (Eds.), *Handbook of positive psychology* (pp. 257–266). New York: Oxford University Press.

Spreitzer, G., & Sonenshein, S. (2003). Positive deviance and extraordinary organizing. In K.S. Cameron, J.E. Dutton, & R.E. Quinn (Eds.), *Positive organizational scholarship: Foundations of a new discipline* (pp. 207–224). San Francisco, CA: Berrett-Koehler.

Sternberg, R.J. (1988). *The triangle of love: Intimacy, passion, commitment*. New York: Basic Books.

Suh, E., Diener, E., & Fujuta, F. (1996). Events and subjective well-being: Only recent events matter. *Journal of Personality and Social Psychology*, 70, 1091–1102.

Sullivan, O., & Gershuny, J. (2001). Cross-national changes in time-use: Some sociological (hi)stories re-examined. *British Journal of Sociology*, 52, 331–347.

Teasdale, J.D., Segal, Z.V., Williams, J.M.G., Ridgeway, V., Lau, M., & Soulsby, J. (2000). Reducing risk of recurrence of major depression using mindfulness-based cognitive therapy. *Journal of Consulting and Clinical Psychology*, 68, 615–623.

Tedeschi, R.G., & Calhoun, L.G. (2004). A clinical approach to posttraumatic growth. In P.A. Linley & S. Joseph (Eds.) *Positive psychology in practice* (pp. 405–419). Hoboken, NJ: Wiley.

Tennen, H., & Affleck, G. (2002). Benefit-finding and benefit-reminding. In C.R. Snyder & S.J. Lopez (Eds.), *Handbook of positive psychology* (pp. 584–597). New York: Oxford University Press.

Tennen, H., & Affleck, G. (2003). While accentuating the positive, don't eliminate the negative or Mr. In-Between. *Psychological Inquiry, 14*, 163–169.

Toffler, A. (1970). *Future shock.* London: Pan Books.

Tyrrell, B. (1995). Time in our lives: Facts and analysis on the 90s. *Demos, 5*, 23–25.

Vaillant, G. (2000). Adaptive mental mechanisms: Their role in positive psychology. *American Psychologist, 55*, 89–98.

Vaillant, G.R. (2004). Positive aging. In P.A. Linley and S. Joseph (Eds.), *Positive psychology in practice* (pp. 561–578). Hoboken, NJ: Wiley.

Veenhoven, R. (1991). Is happiness relative? *Social Indicators Research, 24*, 1–34.

Veenhoven, R. (2000). The four qualities of life: Ordering concepts and measures of the good life. *Journal of Happiness Studies, 1*, 1–39.

Vittersø, J. (2003). Flow versus life satisfaction: A projective use of cartoons to illustrate the difference between the evaluation approach and the intrinsic motivation approach to subjective quality of life. *Journal of Happiness Studies, 4*, 141–167.

Vittersø, J. (undated). Stability and change: Integrating hedonism and eudaimonism into a model of dynamic well-being. Unpublished manuscript.

Vittersø, J., Søholt, Y., Hetland, A., Thoresen, I.A., & Røysamb, E. (2010). Was Hercules happy? Some answers from a functional model of human well-being. *Social Indicators Research, 95*, 1–18.

Waterman, A.S. (1993). Two conceptions of happiness: Contrasts of personal expressiveness (eudaimonia) and hedonic enjoyment. *Journal of Personality and Social Psychology, 64*, 678–691.

Waterman, A.S. (2008). Reconsidering happiness: A eudaimonist's perspective. *Journal of Positive Psychology, 3*, 234–252.

Waterman, A.S., Schwartz, S.J., Goldbacher, E., Green, H., Miller, C., & Philip, S. (2003). Predicting the subjective experience of intrinsic motivation: The roles of self-determination, the balance of challenges and skills, and self-realization values. *Personality and Social Psychology Bulletin, 29*, 1447–1458.

Whitmore, J. (1997). *Need, greed and freedom.* Shaftesbury, UK: Element Books.

Williamson, G.M. (2002). Aging well. In C.R. Snyder & S.J. Lopez (Eds.), *Handbook of positive psychology* (pp. 676–686). New York: Oxford University Press.

Wills, T.A., Sandy, J.M., & Yaeger, A.M. (2001). Time perspective and early-onset substance use: A model based on stress-coping theory. *Psychology of Addictive Behaviours, 15*, 118–125.

Worsley, R., & Joseph, S. (2005). Shared roots. *Counselling and Psychotherapy Journal, 16*(5), 24–26.

Young-Eisendrath, P. (2003). Response to Lazarus. *Psychological Inquiry, 14*, 170–173.

Zaleski, Z., Cycon, A., & Kurc, A. (2001). Future time perspective and subjective well-being in adolescent samples. In P. Schmuck & K.M. Sheldon (Eds.), *Life goals and well-being: Towards a positive psychology of human striving* (pp. 58–67). Göttingen: Hogrefe & Huber.

Zimbardo, P.G. (2002). Just think about it: Time to take our time. *Psychology Today, 35*, 62.

Zimbardo, P.G., & Boyd, J.N. (1999). Putting time in perspective: A valid, reliable individual-differences metric. *Journal of Personality and Social Psychology, 77*, 1271–1288.

Zullow, H., Oettingen, G., Peterson, C., & Seligman, M.E.P. (1988). Pessimistic explanatory style in the historical record: CAVing LBJ, Presidential candidates and East versus West Berlin. *American Psychologist, 43*, 673–682.

Index

Locators shown in *italics* refer to student goals, tables, and tips and tools.

acceptance, partner
  feature of minding model of love, 127–8
accomplishment
  salience in authentic happiness model, 55
achievement
  as element of time management, 80–81
  as personal strength, 111
  as value driving well-being, 64
actions, human
  as feature of flow, 30
  broadening of by positive emotions, 10
Action for Happiness, 170
activation
  as personal strength, 112
actualization
  salience for humanistic psychology,
    50–51
adaptability
  as personal strength, 112
  features and role of defence, 84–5
adaptation theory
  application to happiness, 42
addiction
  salience as danger of flow, 34–5
adversity
  approaches to challenge of, 83–7
affect
  characteristics and role in notion of
    SWB, 41
  definition, 9
  see also emotions, negative; emotions,
    positive; intelligence, emotional

Affllek, G., 163, 166
affluence, time
  tips and tools on importance, 78
agape
  features and salience as love type, 123
age and ageing
  salience of positivity towards challenge
    of, 89–92
AI (appreciative inquiry)
  process and role in positive psychology,
    158–9
Allport, G., 6, 49
analysis
  as personal strength, 112
Anderson, E., 104, 110–14, *111–13*
anxieties
  as element of time management, 81
  implications for loving relationships,
    121–2
  reduction of as positive psychology
    intervention, 141
  relationship with values and happiness,
    64–5
apathy
  tips on moving away from, 33
appreciative inquiry (AI)
  process and role in positive psychology,
    158–9
Aristippus, 50
Aristotle, 5, 50, 61
arrangement
  as personal strength, 112

Art of Loving (Fromm), 129
assurance, self-
  as personal strength, 113
attachment theory
  application to concept of love, 120–22
attitude
  salience in post-traumatic growth, 86
attributes, partner
  feature of minding model of love, 127
authentic happiness (concept)
  application to happiness and well-being,
    55
  website of organization, 170
autonomy
  implications for loving relationships,
    121
  salience as feature of POS, 157
  salience for intrinsic motivation, 66–7
  situational overview and threats, 95–8
  see also outcomes of e.g. overchoice
autopilot
  feature of SPARK Resilience programme,
    150–51
autotelic personality (concept)
  application to happiness and well-being,
    53–4, 54
  definition, 33
avoidance
  implications for loving relationships, 122
  salience is coping strategy, 84
awareness, emotional
  merging and loss as feature of flow, 30
  tips and tools for self-monitoring of,
    16–17

balance (concept)
  as element of time management, 80
  need for in contribution of TP to well-
    being, 77–8
  need for rectification of lack of, 165–7
  role in Sternberg's theory of wisdom,
    88–9
Bandura, A., 65
Baylis, N., 151
behaviours, learned
  salience in relation to strengths, 114–15

beliefs
  as personal strength, 111
benevolence
  salience as value driving well-being, 64
Ben-Shahar, T., 137–8, 141–2
Berlin's wisdom paradigms, 87–8
bias, temporal
  tips and tools on reducing, 77
blame, self
  salience as cost of maximization, 99
Bonanno, T., 13
Bounce Back programme, 149
'Broaden and Build' theory of positive
  emotions, 10
Brown, K., 67
Bryant, F., 136

Carr, A., 22, 28, 48
Centre for Applied Positive Psychology
  (CAPP), 114–15, 171
Centre for Confidence and Wellbeing, 170
Centre for Positive Organizational
  Scholarship, 171
children
  tips for developing motivation in, 67
choice (concept)
  role in happiness and well-being, 59
  situational overview and threats,
    95–8
  see also overchoice
classifications and typologies
  of strengths and virtues, 105–15, 107–9,
    111–13
  positive psychology, 2
Clifton, D., 104, 110–14, *111–13*
coaching
  comparison with therapy, 144–6
  features and link with positive
    psychology, 143–4, 146–7
  see also education; therapy
command
  as personal strength, 111
communication
  as personal strength, 112
community
  features as level of positive psychology, 3

companionship
    as positive psychology intervention, 140
compassion
    salience as love feature, 124–5
competitiveness
    as personal strength, 112
concentration
    as characteristic of flow, 30
conflict, goal
    tips and tools for managing, 69
confidence
    feature of positive organizations, 154
conformity
    salience as value driving well-being, 64
connectedness
    as personal strength, 113
    salience of high-quality in POS, 157
consciousness, self-
    loss of as feature of flow, 30
consistency
    as personal strength, 113
contempt, personal
    as indicator of likely divorce, 126
contextualization
    as personal strength, 113
continuity
    feature of minding model of love, 128
control
    role of emotional in happiness and well-
        being, 60
    salience of lack of as element of time
        management, 81
    sense of as feature of flow, 31
coping, adversity
    characteristics of strategies, 83–4
costs, opportunity
    as cost of maximization, 99
countries and cultures
    experiences of flow, 32–3
courage
    salience as strength and virtue, 106,
        108
courses, education
    within positive psychology field, 149–53
creativity
    feature of positive organizations, 154–5

criticism
    style of as indicator of likely divorce, 126
Csikszentmihalyi, M., 29– 31, 33, 34, 35,
    53–4, 76, 155–6, 166
cultures and countries
    experiences of flow, 32–3

Deci, E., 53
defensiveness
    fact of as indicator of likely divorce, 126
deliberation
    as personal strength, 113
demonstrativeness
    as positive psychology intervention, 140
De Shazer, S., 148–9
designer
    as stage of AI, 158
destiny
    as stage of AI, 158
determination, self-
    theory of, 53, 65–6
    website on, 170
development, self-
    as personal strength, 113
    enhancement of by positive emotions, 12
    role in happiness and well-being, 58–60
development, personal
    tips for work out of, 59
deviance, positive
    salience in POS, 157
Diener, E., 24, 45
direction, self-
    as feature of POS, 157
    as value driving well-being, 64
discipline
    as personal strength, 113
discovery
    as stage of AI, 158
dismissiveness
    implications for loving relationships, 122
divorce, matrimonial
    indicators of likelihood, 125–6
    tips and tools on ways of incurring, 126
dreams and dreaming
    as stage of AI, 158
Dweck, C 116–17

education
  positive psychology programmes,
    149–53
Ehrenreich, B., 24, 164–5
Emotional Intelligence (Goleman), 15
emotions
  definition, 9
  see also intelligence, emotional
emotions, negative
  need for positive psychology appreciation
    of, 165
  positive impact of, 13–15
  role of positive emotion in undoing,
    10–11
emotions, positive
  as personal strength, 113
  need for positive psychology
    consideration of, 164–5
  salience in authentic happiness model,
    55
  salience of focusing on as coping strategy,
    83
  value, importance and benefits, 9–13,
    11
  see also intelligence, emotional
empathy
  as personal strength, 113
engagement
  salience in authentic happiness model, 55
EQ (emotional intelligence)
  characteristics and model, 15–18, 15
  educational programmes involving,
    149–50
Eros
  features and salience as love type, 123
errors, of judgement
  problems posed by choices availability, 97
eudaimonism
  application to psychological well-being,
    51–6, 52, 54, 56, 58–61
  definition and characteristics, 57–8
European Network of Positive Psychology,
    169
exercise
  as positive psychology intervention,
    137–8

expectations
  escalation of as cost of maximization, 99
experiences, optimal
  flow of life as, 29–35, 33, 34
  Maslow's peak experience as, 35–6
explanation, pessimistic
  tips and tools when disputing, 22
expressiveness, personal
  application to happiness and well-being,
    54–5
external motivation
  salience in driving well-being, 66
extrinsic motivation
  characteristics, 65

fatalism, present-
  characteristics as subtype of time
    perspective, 74
feedback
  immediacy of as feature of flow, 30
findings, research
  need for accurate positive psychology,
    163
flow
  feature of positive organizations, 155–6
'flow', of life
  dangers of 34–5
  definition and characteristics, 29–30
  process of making it happen, 30–34, 33,
    34
Flow: the Psychology of Happiness
    (Csikszentmihalyi), 29
focus
  as personal strength, 111
forgiveness
  feature of minding model of love, 128–9
Frankl, V., 86
Fredrickson, B., 10–12, 13, 140
freedom
  situational overview and threats, 95–8
  see also outcomes e.g. overchoice
Fromm, E., 68, 129
functional well-being
  application to happiness and well-being,
    55–7, 56
Future Shock (Toffler), 95–6, 100

Gable, S., 134
Gallup Corporation, 110–13, *111–13*
Gallup foundation, 149, 155
goals, life
    clarity of personal as feature of flow, 30
    definition, characteristics and role in
        well-being, 67–8
    tips and tools for managing conflict of, 69
    types enabling happiness and well-being,
        68–70
Going for the Goal programme, 149
Goleman, D., 15
Gottman, J., 125–6
gratification, delayed
    role in happiness and well-being, 59–60
gratitude
    as positive psychology intervention, 133
'grit,' personal
    role in happiness and well-being, 60
growth, post-traumatic
    features and role in adversity situations,
        85–7

Haberdasher Aske's Academy's Federation,
    152
Happier (Ben-Shahar), 141–2
happiness
    alternatives to hedonic, 50–51
    characteristics and history, 37
    factors enhancing or detracting, 43–6,
        44, 48
    models, theories and approaches, 42–3,
        51–6, 52, 54, 56, 58–61
    problems with existing approaches, 49–50
    questionnaire identifying, 39–40, 40
    reasons for goodness of, 38–9
    those expressing and showing, 38
    websites of research and tests, 169–70
    see also unhappiness; well-being,
        subjective
    see also drivers and contributing factors
        e.g. goals, life; motivations; values
Harker, L., 13
harmony
    salience as personal strength, 112
'hedonic treadmill', 42

hedonism
    alternatives to as approach to happiness,
        50–51
    definition in relation to well-being, 50
    salience as value driving well-being, 64
hedonism, present-
    characteristics as subtype of time
        perspective, 74
Held, B., 164
Henry, J., 154–6
Hertenstein, M., 13
history, roots of
    need for recognition of, 162
history (life history)
    summarising of as positive psychology
        intervention, 141
hope
    definition, approaches and benefits 27–8,
        28
    questionnaire identifying, 25–6
humanity
    salience as strength and virtue, 106,
        108

ideation
    as personal strength, 111
identified motivation, 66
ideology
    need for balanced positive psychology,
        164
image, self-
    as positive psychology intervention,
        138
inclusion
    as personal strength, 111
individuality
    as personal strength, 112
    features as level of positive psychology,
        3
information
    problems posed by choices availability,
        97
input
    as personal strength, 112
integrated motivation
    salience in driving well-being, 66

intellection
  as personal strength, 112
intelligence, emotional
  characteristics and model, 15–18, 15
  educational programmes involving,
    149–50
International Positive Psychology
  Association (IPPA), 169
internet
  websites of organizations, 169–71
interventions, psychology
  evidence-based supporting positivity,
    132–9
  untested supporting positivity, 139–42
intrinsic motivation
  characteristics, 65
  feature of positive organizations, 154
  salience of autonomy, 66–7
  tips and tools for awakening and
    enhancing, 65, 66
introjected motivation
  salience in driving well-being, 66
IPPA (International Positive Psychology
  Association), 169

Jahoda, M., 6
Jenkins, J., 9
jobs
  variety of as feature of positive
    organizations, 154
judgement, individual
  problems posed by choices availability,
    97
Jung, C., 6, 49
justice
  salience as strength and virtue, 106,
    108
Jyengar, S., 97–8

Kabat-Zinn, J., 153
Kahneman, D., 41
Kasser, T., 78
Keltner, D., 13
kindness
  as positive psychology intervention,
    133

knowledge
  feature of SPARK Resilience programme,
    150–51
  salience as strength and virtue, 106, 107
knowledge, partner
  feature of minding model of love, 127

Lane, R., 72
Lazarus, R., 165–6
leadership, positive
  salience in POS, 157–8
Learned Optimism (Seligman), 21
learning
  as personal strength, 112
Lepper, M., 97–8
life, flow of
  dangers of 34–5
  definition and characteristics, 29–30
  process of making it happen, 30–34, 33,
    34
life, satisfaction with (SWL)
  characteristics and context, 41–2, 61
  connection with TP and maximization,
    78, 100
Little, B., 61
Locke, J., 50
Lopez, S., 26, 27
love
  indicators of divorce from, 125–6
  models, theories and styles, 120–25,
    127–9
  place within positive psychology, 119–20
  salience as strength and virtue, 106, 108
ludus
  features and salience as love type, 123
Lyubomirsky, S., 48, 70, 139

McGrath, H., 149
McGregor, I., 61
Making Hope Happen programme, 149
management, emotional
  as element of Mayer-Salovey-Caruso
    model, 17–18, 17
  tips and tools for, 17
management, time
  importance and principles, 79–81

mania
  features and salience as love type, 123
Man's Search for Meaning (Frankl), 86
manuals
  of strengths and virtues, 105–15, 107–9,
    111–13
  positive psychology, 2
Maslow, A., 6, 35–6, 49, 50, 76
maximizers and maximization
  as personal strength, 112
  definition and role of choice for, 98–9
  weaknesses of trap of, 99–100, 100
Mayer-Salovey-Caruso model of emotional
    intelligence, 15, 16–18
MBCT (Mindfulness-Based Cognitive
    Therapy), 152–3
meaning, pleasure, strengths (MPS)
  process as positive psychology
    intervention, 141–2
meaningfulness
  as feature of POS, 157
  salience in authentic happiness model, 55
mechanisms, defence
  features and role in adversity situations,
    84–5
metaperspective
  feature of positive organizations, 155
methodology, research
  need for appropriate, 163
mindfulness
  tips about concept today, 153
Mindfulness-Based Cognitive Therapy
    (MBCT), 152–3
minding model of relationship
    development, 127–9
mindsets
  characteristics of theory of, 116–17
Mischel, W., 60
models and theories
  emotional intelligence, 15
  eudaimonic well-being, 51–61, 52, 54, 56
  mindsets, 116–17
  motivation and life goals, 65–6, 67–8
  of love, 120–25, 127–9
  positive emotions, 10–12
  raising subjective well-being, 42–3

role of wisdom in positive psychology,
    87–9
monitoring, self-
  for emotional awareness, 16–17
Morris, I., 151
motivation
  as element of time management, 79–80
  definition, features and role in well-being,
    65–7
  see also type e.g. intrinsic motivation
MPS (meaning, pleasure, strengths)
  process as positive psychology
    intervention, 141–2
Myers, D., 48

negativism, emotional
  need for positive psychology appreciation
    of, 165
  positive impact of, 13–15
  role of positive emotion in undoing,
    10–11
negativism, past-
  characteristics as subtype of time
    perspective, 74
New Economics Foundation, 171
Noble, P., 149

Oatley, K., 9
Oishi, S., 68
one-sidedness
  need for rectification of, 165–7
openness
  feature of positive organizations, 156
optimism
  definition, characteristics and need for,
    19–20
  styles and process of learning, 21–3, 22
  see also hope; pessimism; realism
opportunities
  salience as cost of maximization, 99
organizational scholarship, positive, 156–8
organizations, positive
  practices and interventions, 154–6
  see also tools used e.g. appreciative
    inquiry; positive organizational
    scholarship

organizations, psychology
  websites of, 169–71
orientation (future orientation)
  as personal strength, 112
  characteristics as subtype of time
    perspective, 74
overchoice
  personality responses to problem of,
    98–100, 100
  situational overview and threats, 96–8
  solutions to problem of, 100–101

paradigms
  Berlin's wisdom, 87–8
participation
  feature of positive organizations, 156
passion
  salience as love feature, 124–5
peak experience (Maslow), 35–6
Penn Resiliency Programme (PRP), 149–50
perceptions
  as element of Mayer-Salovey-Caruso
    model, 15, 16
  feature of SPARK Resilience programme,
    150–51
personal expressiveness (concept)
  application to happiness and well-being,
    54–5
personality
  extent of influence on happiness, 45
perspective (time perspective)
  contribution to well-being, 76–8
  definition and characteristics, 73–5
pessimism
  definition, 19
  situations when pessimism is good, 23–4
  styles and tips and tools, 22
  see also hope; optimism; realism
Peterson, C., 105–10, 107–9
philia
  features and salience as love type, 123
pleasurability
  salience in authentic happiness model, 55
Popivic, N., 25, 31, 59, 89
positive organizational scholarship (POS),
  156–8

positive psychology coaching (PPC), 146–7
Positive Psychology Network, 161
Positive Psychology News Daily, 170
positivism, past-
  characteristics as subtype of time
    perspective, 74
positivity, emotional see emotions, positive
power
  salience as value driving well-being, 64
PPC (positive psychology coaching),
  146–7
pragma
  features and salience as love type, 123
preoccupation
  implications for loving relationships,
    121–2
problems
  salience of focusing on as coping strategy,
    83
programmes, education
  within positive psychology field,
    149–53
PRP (Penn Resiliency Programme),
  149–50
psychology
  as element of Mayer-Salovey-Caruso
    model, 15, 16
  broadening of by positive emotions, 10
  enhancement of by positive emotions,
    11–12
psychology, humanistic
  and actualising tendency, 50–51
  see also eudaimonism
psychology, positive
  definition, history and features, 1–2, 2,
    5–7, 7
  education programmes within field,
    149–53
  future prospects, 167–8
  levels of, 3
  reasons for acknowledging, 3–5
  strengths and weaknesses, 161–7
  websites, 169–71
  see also allies e.g. coaching, positive
    psychology; interventions,
    psychology

see also applicable situations and arenas e.g. adversity; age and ageing; employment *see also elements enhancing or detracting e.g.* choice; wisdom
Psychology for Positive Transformation website, 171

Quality-Of-Life therapy, 141
questionnaires
    indications of happiness, 39–40, 40
    meaning of hope, 25–6

reactions
    feature of SPARK Resilience programme, 150–51
Realise2 classification of strengths, 114–15
realism
    importance and need for, 24–5
    positive realism versus realistic optimism, 25
reciprocity
    feature of minding model of love, 128
regret
    as cost of maximization, 99
relationships
    as personal strength, 113
    extent of influence on happiness, 45–6
    salience in authentic happiness model, 55
    see also divorce, matrimonial
reminiscence
    as positive psychology intervention, 138–9
research
    need for accurate methods and findings, 163–4
resilience
    enhancement of by positive emotions, 11
respect, partner
    feature of minding model of love, 127–8
responses, active-constructive
    as positive psychology intervention, 134–5
responsibility
    as element of time management, 80–81
    as personal strength, 113
    role in happiness and well-being, 59

restoration
    as personal strength, 113
reward
    feature of flow, 31
Rogers, C., 6, 49, 50, 51, 58–9, 147
roots, historical
    need for positive psychology recognition of, 162
Ryan, R., 53, 67
Ryff, C., 52–3, *52*, 57, 61, 148

Salovey, P., 15–18, *15*
satisfaction with life (SWL)
    characteristics as element of subjective well-being, 41–2, 61
    connection with TP and maximization, 78, 100
satisficers
    definition and role of choice for, 98–9
savouring
    as positive psychology intervention, 136–7
scales, goal
    on hope, 25–6
Schneider, S., 24–5
scholarship, positive organizational
    definition and link with positive psychology, 156–8
Schwartz, B., 96, 97, 98, 99, 100–101
Schwartz, S., 64
SDT (self-determination theory)
    application to happiness and well-being ideas, 53
    contribution to motivation definitions, 65–6
    websites, 170
security
    salience as value driving well-being, 64
self-concordance model
    contribution to life goal features, 67–8
Self-Determination: the Tyranny of Freedom (Schwartz), 96
self-determination theory (SDT)
    application to happiness and well-being ideas, 53

contribution to motivation definitions,
65–6
websites, 170
Self Science programme, 149
Seligman, M., 1, 4, 21, 29–30, 42–3, 45, 48,
55, 61, 105–10, *107–9*, 161–2
Sheldon, K., 48
significance
as personal strength, 113
situation
feature of SPARK Resilience programme,
150–51
Skills of Well-Being programme, 151–2
Smile or Die (Ehrenreich), 165
Snyder, R., 27
South Africa Emotional Intelligence
Curriculum, 149
SPARK Resilience Programme, 150–51
standardization
response to overchoice, 98
Sternberg, R., 88–9, 122, 123, 149
Sternberg's balance theory of wisdom, 88–9
stimulation
salience as value driving well-being, 64
stonewalling
fact of as indicator of likely divorce, 126
storge
features and salience as love type, 123
Strange Situation Test, 120–21
strategies, coping
features and role in adversity situations,
83–4
strategy
as personal strength, 113
strengths, personal
characteristics and classifications, 105–
15, *107–9*, *111–13*
feature of positive organizations, 155
identification and action as positive
psychology intervention, 135–6
personality implications of focusing on,
115–17
tips and tools for discovering and
applying, 114
value to positive psychology, 103–4
StrengthsFinder (Gallup), 110–13, *111–13*

StrengthsQuest, 170
subjective well-being *see* well-being,
subjective
subjectivity
features as level of positive psychology, 3
summarization, life history
as positive psychology intervention, 141
support, interpersonal
salience in post-traumatic growth, 86
SWB *see* well-being, subjective
SWL (satisfaction with life)
characteristics as element of subjective
well-being, 41–2, 61
connection with TP and maximization,
78, 100

talents *see* strengths, personal
teams, building of
feature of positive organizations, 155
temperance
salience as strength and virtue, 106, 108
Tennen, H., 163, 166
theories *see* models and theories
theory, research
need to guide positive psychology, 163
therapy
characteristics of positive, 147–9
comparison with coaching, 144–6
see also particular e.g. Mindfulness-Based
Cognitive Therapy
thoughts and thinkingl
as element of Mayer-Salovey-Caruso
model, 15, 16
broadening of by positive emotions, 10
enhancement of by positive emotions,
11–12
thoughts and thinking, humanistic
and actualising tendency, 50–51
see also eudaimonism
thoughts and thinking, positive *see*
psychology, positive
'three good things' positive psychology
intervention, 132–3, 141–2
time
as positive psychology intervention,
140–41

changing nature of uses, 71–3
importance and principles of
    management of, 79–81
salience as cost of maximization, 99
transformation of as feature of flow, 31
see also management, time
time perspective (TP)
connection with SWB, 78
contribution to well-being, 76–8
definition and characteristics, 73–5
tips and tools
awakening and enhancing intrinsic
    motivation, 65, 66
daimon in action, 51
developing integrated motivation in
    children, 67
discovering and applying personal
    strengths, 114
emotional management, 17
getting rid of temporal biases, 77
importance of time affluence, 78
managing goal conflict, 69
mindfulness today, 153
moving from apathy to 'flow', 33
personal development work out, 59
positive realism versus realistic optimism,
    25
process of generating hope, 28
process of identifying 'flow', 34
self-monitoring for emotional awareness,
    16–17
ways of destroying relationship, 126
when disputing pessimistic explanation,
    22
wisdom awakening, 89
Toffler, A., 95–6, 98, 100, 167
TP (time perspective)
connection with SWB, 78
contribution to well-being, 76–8
definition and characteristics, 73–5
tradition
salience as value driving well-being, 64
transcendence
as strength and virtue, 106, 109
role in happiness and well-being, 58–60
Triangle of Love (Sternberg), 122

triangular theory
application to concept of love, 122–3
typologies and classifications
of strengths and virtues, 105–15, 107–9,
    111–13
positive psychology, 2

understanding, of emotions
as element of Mayer-Salovey-Caruso
    model, 15, 16
unhappiness
groups showing, 36
universalism
salience as value driving well-being, 64
University of East London, 152, 170
University of Rochester, 170

Vaillant, G., 90–91
value-as-a-moderator model
salience in relation to life goals, 68
values
definition, characteristics and role in
    well-being, 63–5
variety, job
feature of positive organizations, 154
Veroff, J., 136
VIA Classification of Strengths and Virtues,
    105–10, 107–9
virtues
characteristics and classifications, 105–
    10, 107–9
personality implications of focusing on,
    115–17
Vittersø, J., 55–6

Ward, A., 99, 100–101
warmth, personal
as positive psychology intervention, 140
Waterman, A., 54–5, 51
weaknesses
salience in relation to strengths, 114–15
well-being, psychological
contribution of time perspective to, 76–8
eudaimonic theories of, 51–7, 52, 54, 56,
    58–61
see also happiness; unhappiness

see also drivers and contributing factors e.g. goals, life; motivations; values
well-being, subjective
definition and characteristics, 40–42
factors enhancing or detracting from, 46–7
theories of methods of raising, 42–3
see also happiness; unhappiness
Well-Being Curriculum, 152
Well-being Institute, 171
Wellington College (UK), 151–2
Williamson, G., 90
wisdom
features and role in adversity situations, 87–9

salience as strength and virtue, 106, 107
tips and tools for awakening, 89
Wisdom Curriculum programme, 149
'woo'
as personal strength, 113
workplaces
role and importance of positive psychology, 154–9
World Wide Web
websites of organizations, 169–71
worries *see* anxieties

zero–sum theory
application to happiness, 42

UNDERSTANDING YOUR EATING
How to Eat and not Worry About it

Julia Buckroyd

9780335241972 (Paperback)
2011

eBook also available

"To understand your eating, you first have to understand yourself. This easily-read book helps you to step back and discover what influences your eating habits."
Dr Ian Campbell – Founder of the National Obesity Forum and medical consultant on ITV's The Biggest Loser and Fat Chance

"This valuable book makes sense of how food and eating may be misused and become entangled with emotions as a way of dealing with them."
Dr Helena Fox – Clinical psychiatrist for Channel 4's Supersize vs Superskinny and for the eating disorders unit at Capio Nightingale Hospital

Key features:

- Thoroughly updates and revises the hugely popular book, Eating Your Heart Out
- The author runs a national network of workshops and seminars in this area
- Provides a wealth of practical advice on how to tackle the problem

www.openup.co.uk

POSITIVE PSYCHOLOGY
Theory, Research and Applications

Kate Hefferon and Ilona Boniwell

9780335241958 (Paperback)
June 2011

eBook also available

"Kate Hefferon and Ilona Boniwell have done an excellent job on this introduction to Positive Psychology! I encourage educators, students and everyone else interested in an updated, well-written and culturally balanced approach to the scientific study of human flourishing, to read this highly accessible, yet rigorously crafted text; and to get it under your skin by ways of carefully chosen tests and exercises."
Hans Henrik Knoop, Aarhus University, Denmark and President, European Network for Positive Psychology

This new textbook combines a breadth of information about positive psychology with reflective questions, critical commentary and up to date research.

Key features:

- Contains personal development exercises to help meld together research and application
- Experiments boxes detail the most influential positive psychology experiments to date
- Measurement tools presenting popular positive psychology tools

www.openup.co.uk

OPEN UNIVERSITY PRESS
McGraw · Hill Education